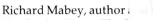

Richard Mabey, author ⋯ ⋯ ⋯ or
The Sunday Times, The S⋯ ⋯ ⋯ ⋯nt.
He won wide acclaim on the publication of the original *Food for Free* in 1972, and in 1986 was awarded the Whitbread Prize for Biography for *Gilbert White, A Biography*. He is an active member of national and local conservation groups and lives in Hertfordshire.

Richard Mabey

FOOD FOR FREE

COLLINS
8 Grafton Street, London W1

William Collins Sons & Co. Ltd
London · Glasgow · Sydney · Auckland
Toronto · Johannesburg

First Published 1972
Reprinted January 1973
Reprinted August 1973
Reprinted November 1973
Reprinted February 1974
Reprinted December 1974
Reprinted 1976
Reprinted 1977
Reprinted 1978
Reprinted 1980
First Published in this all-colour edition 1989

ISBN 0 00 219856 8   Hardback

ISBN 0 00 219865 7   Paperback

Designer: Glynis Edwards

Printed and bound in Italy by
New Interlitho SpA, Milan

CONTENTS

For My Mother

PREFACE
TO THE NEW EDITION

The first edition of *Food for Free* was published in 1972, at just about the same time as the issues of food quality and the environment were beginning to become matters of public concern. Since then an interest in edible wild plants has, dare one say, mushroomed. A huge amount of old knowledge has been re-discovered. Wild plants have become touchstones against which to measure the nutritional content of cultivated varieties, and the inspiration for new crops. The whole subject has lost the slight note of eccentricity it had in the early 70s, and the need for a new edition to take account of all these changes was clear.

Thankfully, perhaps, there have been less serious developments, too. Foraging has become an acceptable family pastime again. Wild vegetable seeds are back on the market – in the case of some varieties, for the first time in three centuries. And in new wave restaurants throughout the countryside, samphire, bistort, oyster mushrooms are beginning to appear on the menus.

To the cynical the whole business still seems trivial and self-deluding, a fashionable pretence at primitivism. Yet more generously it could be seen as a natural outcome of the ecological concerns and longings of the last decade. The hundreds of letters sent to me by readers suggest not so much a misty nostalgia for the simple life, as a growing awareness of how food fits into the whole living scheme of things, and a deepening respect for the ingenuity of our ancestors. They suggest a very active readership, too. Readers have written about brewing wild raspberry vinegar long before it became a fashionable ingredient of *nouvelle cuisine*, about the secret sites and local names of the little wild damsons that grow on the Essex borders, about childhood feasts of seaweed 'boiled in burn water and laid on dog rose bushes to dry'. In Milden, Suffolk, the inhabitants have commemorated the discovery that their village name derives from the prehistoric staple vegetable fat hen (*melde* in Old English). At the village boundary a huge cast iron statue of the plant now overlooks fields where fat hen itself survives amongst the sugar beet.

There have been adventurous experiments as well as historical unearthings. Gadgets for gathering hazel nuts and bilberries have been invented or revived. An agricultural researcher in Berkshire has been working on the use of lady's bedstraw as a source of vegetarian rennet. Foreign cuisines – Asian especially – in which wild plants have always played an important role have been brought to bear on our native wildings. And there have been multitudes of experiments with fruit liqueurs some way beyond sloe gin: service berries in malt whisky, damsons in brandy, cloudberries in aquavit.

It is the changed attitude towards fungi which has perhaps been the decisive sign. Until very recently we seemed to be as suspicious of toadstools as Francis Bacon, who in 1627 dismissed the entire tribe as 'a venereous meat'. But things changed dramatically in the autumn of 1976, the year of the Great Drought and an *annus mirabilis* for mushrooms. When the rains came in September the growth of the underground network of fungal 'roots', starved and stressed by the drought, was so astonishing that it could be smelt in the air after the downpours. When the fruiting began a short while after it was, as usual, the continental immigrants who were first on the scene (some Polish friends in my home town picked 50 lbs of ceps in a single afternoon). But, with an enthusiasm that would have been unthinkable a decade before, the natives were close behind. There was something very close to queuing in the best fungal woods. In the fields, foraging for field and horse mushrooms became a national pastime, and the BBC began running information bulletins. By the end of the month the wild mushroom mountain was so huge they were being given away in pubs, and two nine-year-olds came down our road one afternoon hawking them at 10p a pound.

Now even English truffle-hunting is being revived, and there is a growing affection for the giant puffball, voted the star wild food by most of those who've tried it. I am regularly sent photographs of five-pounders or more, posed on bars or alongside children or cats, as if they were a species of pet themselves.

One misconception about the book has been decisively challenged, too. *Food for Free* was never intended to be a survival manual, and wild plants would not be a very practicable way of staying alive, except in the short term. I was delighted to hear about the young boy who survived being lost in the Cairngorms for more than a week by munching nothing more than bilberries and cowberries, and from the group of art students who eked out a summer grant by using the book as if it were the parable of loaves and fishes. But when the BBC marooned a group of volunteers on Exmoor for the two most fruitful weeks one autumn to live off the wild, they each lost nearly a stone in weight, and I watched them walk off the moor in slow motion, dreaming of Mars bars.

Playing at survival is, I feel, the unacceptable face of foraging, smacking of SAS endurance tests and often leading to wilful callousness – 'a Man's Life' more than the Good Life. I heard from a science master at Gordonstoun who, true to the spartan spirit of his school, had taken a party of boys on a 'survival expedition' to Cape Wrath and had eaten 'considerable numbers of the large seashore woodlouse . . . frogs and common toads (rather tough and stringy but wholesome)'. (Though a short while later another schoolmaster – Eton, this time – told me of a blow struck back by nature in its continuing war with the public school male. His Scottish cottage, where he keeps a copy of *Food for Free*, is empty most of the year, except for the mice 'which come in for comfort and culture'. That spring they came in for rather more, and taking the book's title at face value began eating chunks out of the dust-jacket.)

What has emerged from most readers' letters is an altogether more gentle and compassionate attitude. It is the *intimacy* with wild things that foraging can bring that seems to be most richly enjoyed. I can say this with some feeling myself, being less of an intensive gatherer these days than a devotee of the wayside nibble, in what the 1930s fruit gourmet Edward Bunyard called 'ambulant consumption'!

This new edition, as well as being thoroughly revised, made less parochial and having its recipes brought into line with modern nutritional ideas, includes many of the insights and practical discoveries of readers and friends, and I must extend my warmest thanks to all those who have written to me over the past years. It is their book as much as mine – though any mistakes and moments of tastelessness are, of course, purely my responsibility.

Richard Mabey, Berkhamsted, 1988.

INTRODUCTION

It is easy to forget, as one stands before the modern supermarket shelf, that every single one of the world's vegetable foods was once a wild plant. What we buy and eat today is nothing more special than the results of generations of plant-breeding experiments. Most of these were directed towards improving size and cropping ability. Some were concerned with flavour and texture – but these are fickle qualities, dependent for their popularity as much on fashion as on any inherent virtue. Lately there have been more ominous moves towards improving colour and shape.

Yet if plant breeding has been directed towards the introduction of bland, inoffensive flavours, and has sacrificed much for the sake of convenience, those old robust tastes, the curly roots and fiddle-some leaves, are still there for the enjoyment of those who care to seek them out. Almost every British garden vegetable (greenhouse species excepted) still has a wild ancestor flourishing here. Wild cabbages grow along the south coast, celery along the east. Wild parsnips flourish on waste ground everywhere. In times of scarcity they are turned to again, yet each time with less ingenuity and confidence, less native knowledge about what they are and how they can be used.

Food for Free is about these plants, and how they once were and can still be used as food. It is a practical book, I hope, but not an urgent one. It would be foolish to pretend that there are any press-ing economic reasons why we should have a large scale revival of wild food use. You would need to be a most determined picker to keep yourself alive on wild vegetables, and since they are so easy to cultivate there would be very little point in trying. Nor are wild fruits and vegetables necessarily more healthy and nutritious than cultivated varieties – though some are, and most of them are likely to be comparatively free of herbicides and other agricultural pois-ons.

Why bother then? Why not leave wild food utterly to the birds and slugs? My initial pleas are, I'm afraid, almost purely sensual and indulgent: interest, experience, and even, on a small scale, adven-ture. The history of wild food use is interesting enough in its own right, and those who would never dream of grubbing about on a damp woodland floor for their supper may still find themselves impressed by our ancestors' resourcefulness. But those who are prepared to venture out will find more substantial rewards. It is the flavours and textures that will surprise the most, I think, and the realisation of to just what extent the cultivation and mass production of food have muted our taste experiences. There is a whole galaxy of powerful and surprising flavours preserved intact in the wild stock, that are quite untapped in cultivated foods: tart and smoky berries, aromatic fungi, crisp and succulent shoreline plants.

There is much along these lines that could be said in favour of wild foods. Some of them are delicacies, many of them are still abundant, and all of them are free. They require none of the attention demanded by garden plants, and possess the additional attraction of having to be *found*. I think I would rate this as perhaps the most attractive single feature of wild food use. The satisfactions of cultivation are slow and measured. They are not at all like the excitement of raking through a rich bed of cockles, of suddenly discovering a clump of sweet cicely, of tracking down a bog myrtle by its smell alone. There is something akin to hunting here: the search, the gradually acquired wisdom about seasons and habitats, the satisfaction of having proved you can provide for yourself. What you find may make no more than an intriguing addition to your normal diet, but it was you that found it. And in coastal areas, in a good autumn, it could be a whole three-course meal.

WILD FOOD AND NECESSITY

It is not easy to tell how wide a range of plants was eaten before agriculture began. The seeds of any number of species have been found in neolithic settlements, but these may have already been under a primitive system of cultivation. Plants gathered from the wild would inevitably drop their seed and begin to grow near their pickers' dwellings; and if, as was likely, the specimens collected were above average in size or yield, so might be their offspring. So a sort of automatic selection would have taken place, with crops of the more fruitful plants growing naturally near habitation.

By the Elizabethan era, the range of wild plants and herbs used and understood by the average cottager was wide and impressive. In many ways it had to be. There was no other source of readily available medicine and of cultivated vegetables. Yet even under conditions of necessity, how is one to explain the discovery that as cryptic a part as the *styles* of the saffron crocus were useful as a spice? The number of wild bits and pieces that must have been put to the test in the kitchen at one time or another is hair-raising. We should be thankful the job has been done for us.

Many plants passed into use as food at this time as a by-product of their medicinal use. Blackcurrants, for instance, were certainly used for throat lotions before the recipients realised they were also quite pleasant to eat when you were well. Sheer economy also played a part, as in finding a use for hop tops that had to be thinned out in the spring.

But like so much else, these old skills and customs were eroded by industrialisation and the drift to the towns. The process was especially thorough in the case of wild foods because cultivation brought genuine advances in quality and abundance. But if the knowledge of how to use them was fading, the plants themselves continued to thrive. Most of them prospered as they had always done in woods and hedgerows. Those that flourished best in the human habitats bided their time under fields which had been turned over to cultivation, or moved into the new wasteland habitats that were a by-product of urbanisation. Plants which had been introduced as pot-herbs clung on at the edges of gardens, as persistent as weeds as they were once abundant as vegetables.

Then some crisis would strike the conventional food supplies, and people would be thankful for this persistence. On the island fringes of Britain, where the ground is poor and the weather unpredictably hostile, the tough native plants were the only invariably successful crops. The knowledge of how to use these plants as emergency rations was kept right up to the time air transport provided a reliable lifeline to the mainland.

It was the two World Wars, and the disruptions of food supplies that accompanied them, which provided one of the most striking examples of the usefulness of wild foods. All over occupied Europe fungi were gathered from woods, and wild greens from bomb sites. In America, pilots were given instructions on how to live off the wild in case their planes were ditched over land. And in this country, the government encouraged the 'hedgerow harvest' (as they called one of their publications) as much as the growing of carrots.

Wild plants are invaluable during times of famine or crisis, precisely because they are wild. They are quickly available, tough, resilient, resistant to disease, indifferent for the most part to climate and soil condition. If they were not, they would have simply failed to survive. They are always there, waiting for their moment, thriving under conditions that our pampered cultivated plants would find intolerable.

Some modern agriculturalists are beginning to look seriously at these special qualities of wild food plants. Conventional agriculture works by taking an end food product as given, and modifying plants and conditions of growth to produce it as efficiently as possible. In regions that are vastly different from the plant's natural environment, its survival is always precarious, and often at damaging expense to the soil. The alternative approach is to study the plants that grow naturally and luxuriantly in the area, and see what possible food products can be obtained from them. This looks like being an especially fruitful line of research in developing countries with poor soils.

PLANT USE AND CONSERVATION

These last few instances are examples of conditions in which wild food use was anything but a frivolous pastime. I sincerely hope that this book will never be needed as a manual for that sort of situation. But is there really nothing more to gathering wild foods than the fun of the hunt, and the promise of some exotic new flavours? I think there is. Getting to know these plants and the uses that have been made of them is to begin to understand a whole section of our social history. The plants are a museum in themselves, hangovers from times when palates were less fastidious, living records of famines and changing fashions and even whole peoples. To know their history is to understand how intricately food is bound up with the whole pattern of our social lives. It is easy to forget this by the supermarket shelf, where the food is instantly and effortlessly available, and soil and labour seem part of another existence. We take our food for granted as we do our air and water, and all three are threatened as a result.

Yet familiarity with the ways of just a few of the plants in this book gives an insight at first hand into the complex and delicate relationships which plants have with their environment; their dependence on birds to carry their seeds, animals to crop the grass that shuts out their light, on wind and sunshine and the balance of chemicals in the soil, and ultimately on our own good grace as to whether they survive at all. It is on the products, wild or cultivated, of this intricate network of forces that our food resources depend.

I know there may be some people who will object to this book on the grounds that it may encourage further depletions of our dwindling wild life. I believe that the exact opposite is true. One of the major problems in conservation today is not how to keep people *insulated* from nature but how to help them engage more closely with it, so that they can appreciate its value and vulnerability, and the way its needs can be reconciled with those of humans. One of the most complex and intimate relationships which most of us can have with the natural environment is to eat it. I hope I am not over-stating my case when I say that to follow this relationship through personally, from the search to the cooking pot, is a more practical lesson than most in the economics of the natural world. Far from encouraging rural vandalism, it helps deepen respect for the inter-dependence of all living things. At the very least it will provide a strong motive for looking after particular species and maybe indi-vidual colonies.

OMISSIONS

This book covers the majority of wild plant food products which can be obtained in the British Isles. But there are some categories which I have deliberately omitted.

There is nothing on grasses and cereals. This is intended to be a *practical* book, and no one is going to spend their time hand-gather-ing enough wild seeds to make flour.

I have touched briefly on the traditional herbal uses of many plants where this is relevant or interesting. But I have included no plants purely on the grounds of their presumed therapeutic value. This is a book about food, not medicine.

This is also a book about wild *plant* foods, which is the simple reason (apart from personal qualms) why there is nothing about fish and wildfowl.

But I have included shellfish because from a picker's eye view, they are more like plants than animals. They stay more or less in one place, and are gathered, not caught.

LAYOUT OF THE BOOK

The text and illustrations fall into four sections: edible plants (beginning with trees), seaweeds, fungi and shellfish. Within each category, species are arranged in systematic order.

EDIBLE PLANTS

ROOTS

Roots are probably the least practical of all wild vegetables. Firstly, few species form thick, fleshy roots in the wild, and the coarse, wiry roots of – for instance – horseradish and wild parsnip are really only suitable for flavouring. Second, under the Wildlife and Countryside Act it is illegal to dig up wild plants by the root, except on your own land, or with the permission of the landowner.

The few species that are subsequently recommended as roots are all very common and likely to crop up as garden weeds. Where palatable roots of a practical size and texture can be found, however, they are quite versatile, and may be used in the preparation of broths (see p. 85, herb bennet); vegetable dishes (see p. 95, large evening primrose); salads (see p. 138, ox-eye daisy); or even drinks (see p. 144, chicory).

GREEN VEGETABLES

The main problem with wild leaf vegetables is their *size*. Not many wild plants have the big, floppy leaves for which cultivated greens have been bred, and as a result picking enough for a serving can be a long and irksome task. For this reason the optimum picking time for most leaf vegetables is probably their middle-age, when the flowers are out and the plant is easy to recognise, and the leaves have reached maximum size without beginning to wither.

Green vegetables can be roughly divided into three types: salads, cooked greens, and stems. For general recipes for these categories see: dandelion (p. 145) for salads, sea beet (p. 58) or fat hen (p. 53) for greens, and alexanders (p. 110) for stems.

All green vegetables can also be made into soup (see sorrel, p. 49), blended into green sauces, or made into a pottage or 'mess of greens' by cooking a number of species together.

HERBS

A herb is generally defined as a leafy plant used not as a food in its own right but as a flavouring for other foods, and most herbs tend to be milder in the wild state than under domestication; being valued principally for their flavouring qualities, it is these which domestication has attempted to intensify, not delicacy, size, succulence or any of the other qualities that are sought after in staple vegetables. You will find, consequently, that with wild herbs you will need up to double the quantities you normally use of the cultivated variety.

A few words about the collection, storage and drying of herbs. The best time to pick a herb, especially for the purposes of drying, is just as it is coming into flower. This is the stage at which the plant's nutrients and aromatic oils are still mainly concentrated in the leaves, yet it will have a few blossoms to assist with the identification. Gather your herbs in dry weather and preferably early in the morning before they have been exposed to too much sun. Wet herbs will tend to develop mildew during drying, and specimens picked after long exposure to strong sunshine will inevitably have lost some of their natural oils by evaporation.

Cut whole stalks of the herb with a knife to avoid damaging the parent plant. If you are going to use the herbs fresh, strip the leaves and flowers off the stalks as soon as you get them home. If you are going to dry them, leave the stalks intact as you have picked them. To maintain their colour and flavour they must be dried as quickly as possible but without too intense a heat. They therefore need a combination of gentle warmth and good ventilation. A kitchen or well-ventilated airing cupboard is ideal. The stalks can be hung up in loose bunches, or spread thinly on a sheet of paper and placed on the rack above the stove. Ideally, they should aso be covered by muslin, to keep out flies and insects and, in the case of hanging bundles, to catch any leaves that start to crumble and fall as they dry.

All herbs can be used to flavour vinegar, olive oil or drinks, as with thyme in aquavit.

SPICES

Spices are the aromatic seeds of flowering plants. There are also a few roots (most notably horseradish) that are generally regarded as spices.

Most plants which have aromatic leaves also have aromatic seeds, and can be usefully employed as flavourings. But a warning: do not expect the flavour of the two parts to be identical. They are often subtly different in ways that make it inadvisable simply to substitute seeds for leaves.

Seeds should always be allowed to dry on the plant. After flowering, annuals start to concentrate their food supplies into the seeds so that they have enough to survive through germination. This also, of course, increases the flavour and size of the seeds. When they are dry and ready to drop off the plant, their food content and flavour should be at a maximum.

FLOWERS

Gathering wild flowers for no other reason than their diverting flavours would be anti-social (and, in the case of a few exceptionally rare species, illegal under the Wildlife and Countryside Act).

All the species I have recommended here have certain characteristics which make the picking of their flowers in small quantities unlikely to have much visual or biological effect. They are all very common and hardy plants. They are all perennials and do not rely on seeding for continued survival. They are mostly bushes or shrubs in which each individual produces an abundant number of blossoms.

Most of the recipes on the following pages require no more than a handful or two of blossoms, and most of those flowers mentioned can be used to make salads (see dandelion, p. 145) or flower fritters (see elder, p. 43).

FRUITS

A number of the fruits I have included are cultivated and used commercially as well as growing in the wild. Where this is the case I have not given much space to the more common kitchen uses, which can be found in any cookery book. I have concentrated instead on how to find and gather the wild varieties, and on the more unusual, traditional recipes.

A product that can be made with almost all fruit is, of course, jelly.

Jellies and jams form because of a chemical reaction between a substance called pectin, present in the fruit, and sugar. The pectin (and the fruit's acids, which also play a part in the reaction) tend to be most concentrated when the fruit is under-ripe. But then of course the flavour is only partly developed. So the optimum time for picking fruit for jelly is when it is *just* ripe.

Now the amount of pectin available varies from fruit to fruit. Apples, gooseberries and currants, for instance, are rich in pectin and acid and set very readily. Blackberries and strawberries, on the other hand, have a low pectin content, and usually need to have some added from an outside source before they will form a jelly. Lemon juice or sour crab apples are commonly used for this.

The first stage in making a jelly is to pulp the fruit. Do this by packing the clean fruit into a saucepan or preserving pan and *just* covering with water. Bring to the boil and simmer until all the fruit is mushy. With the harder-skinned fruits (blackcurrants, haws, etc.) you may need to help the process along by pressing with a spoon, and be prepared to simmer for up to half an hour. This is the stage to supplement the pectin, if your fruit has poor setting properties. Add the juice of one lemon for every two lbs (900 gm) of fruit.

Rather than repeat the relevant directions for every entry, I felt it would be simpler to go into some detail here. The notes below apply to all species.

When you have your pulp, separate the juice from the roughage and fibres by straining through muslin. This is most easily done by lining a large bowl with a good-sized sheet of muslin, folded at least double, and filling the bowl with the fruit pulp. Then lift and tie the corners of the muslin, using the back of a chair or a low clothes line as the support, so that it hangs like a sock above the bowl. Alternatively, use a real stocking.

To obtain the maximum volume of juice, allow the pulp to strain overnight. It is not too serious to squeeze the muslin if you are in a hurry, but it will force some of the solid matter through and affect the clarity of your jelly. When you have all the juice you want, measure its volume, and transfer it to a clean saucepan with one lb (453 gm) of preserving sugar for every pint (568 ml) of juice. Bring to the boil, stirring well, and boil rapidly, skimming off any scum that floats to the surface. A jelly will normally form when the mixture has reached a temperature of 221°F (105°C) on a jam thermometer. If you have no thermometer, or want a confirmatory test, transfer one drop of the mixture with a spoon on to a cold saucer. If setting is imminent, the drop will not run after a few seconds because of a skin – often visible – formed across it.

As soon as the setting temperature has been achieved, pour the mixture into some clear, warm jars (preferably standing on a metal surface to conduct away some of the heat). Cover the surface of the jelly with a wax disc, wax side down. Add a cellophane cover, moistening it on the outside first so that it dries taut. Hold the cover in place with a rubber band, label the jar clearly, and store in a cool place.

Another process which can be applied to most of the harder-skinned fruits is drying. Choose slightly unripe fruit, wash well, and dry in a cloth. Then strew it out on a metal tray and place in a very low oven (120°F) (49°C). The fruit is dry when it yields no juice when squeezed between the fingers, but is not so far gone that it rattles. This usually takes between 4 and 6 hours.

Most of the fruits in this section can also be used to make: wine; fruit liqueurs under brandy, gin or aquavit (see sloe gin, p. 41); flavoured vinegars (see raspberry, p. 83); pies, fools; summer or autumn puddings (see blackberry, p. 81).

NUTS

The majority of plants covered by this book are in the 'fruit and veg' category. They make perfectly acceptable accompaniments or conclusions to a meal, but would leave you feeling a little peckish if you relied on nothing else. Nuts are an exception. They are the major source of second-class protein amongst wild plants. Walnuts, for instance, contain 18 per cent protein, 60 per cent fat, and can provide 3000 calories per lb (453 gm) of kernels.

It is therefore possible to substitute nuts for the more conventional protein constituents of a meal – as indeed vegetarians have been doing for centuries. But do not pick them to excess because of this. Wild nuts are crucial to the survival of many wild birds and animals, who have just as much right to them, and considerably more need.

Keep those you do pick very dry, for damp and mould can easily permeate nutshells and rot the kernel.

As well as being edible in their natural state, nuts may be eaten pickled or puréed, mixed into salads, or as a main constituent of vegetable dishes.

SOME PICKING RULES

I have given detailed notes on gathering techniques above and in the introductions to the individual sections (on fungi, etc.). But there are some general rules which apply to all edible plants, and which may help guarantee the quality of what you are picking, and the health of the plant that is providing it.

Although we have tried to make both text and illustrations as helpful as possible in identifying the different plant products described in this book, they should not be regarded as a substitute for a comprehensive field guide. They will help you decide what to gather, but until you are experienced it is wise to double-check everything (particularly fungi) in a book devoted solely to identification. Conversely, never rely on illustrations alone as a guide to edibility. Some of the plants illustrated here need the special preparation described in the text before they are palatable.

But although it is obviously crucial to know what you are picking, don't become obsessed about the possible dangers of poisoning. This is a natural worry when you are trying wild foods for the first time but happily a groundless one. As you will see from the text there are relatively few common poisonous plants in Britain compared with the total number of plant species.

To put the dangers of wild foods into perspective it is worth considering the trials attendant on eating the cultivated foods we stuff into our stomachs without question. Forgetting for a moment the perennial problems of additives and insecticide residues, how many people know that, in excess, cabbage can cause goitre and onions induce anaemia? That as little as one whole nutmeg can bring on days of terrifying hallucinations? Almost any food substance can occasionally bring on an allergic reaction in a susceptible subject, and oysters and strawberries have particularly infamous reputations in this respect. But all these effects are rare. The point is that they are part of the hazards of eating itself, rather than of a particular category of food.

To be doubly sure, it is as well to try fairly small portions of new foods the first time you eat them, just to ensure that you are not sensitive to them.

Having considered your own survival, consider the plant's. Never strip a plant of leaves, berries, or whatever part you are picking. Take small quantities from each specimen, so that its appearance and health are not affected. It helps to use a knife or scissors (except with fungi, see p. 167).

Never take the flowers or seeds of annual plants; they rely on them for survival.

Never pull up whole plants along any path or road verge where the public has access. It is not only anti-social and contrary to all the principles of conservation, but also, in most places, illegal

It is unwise to gather any sorts of produce from areas that may have been sprayed with insecticide or weed killer. Avoid, too, the verges of heavily-used roads, where the plant may have been contaminated by car exhausts. There are plenty of environments that are likely to be comparatively free of all types of contamination: commons, woods, the hedges along footpaths, etc. Even in a small garden you are likely to be able to find something like twenty of the species described in this book.

Wherever possible use a flat open basket to gather your produce, to avoid squashing. If you are caught without a basket, and do not mind being folksy, pin together some dock or burdock leaves with thorns.

When you have got the crop home, wash it well and sort out any old or decayed parts.

TREES

JUNIPER
Juniperus communis

Locally common on chalk downs, limestone hills, heaths and moors, chiefly in South East England and the North.

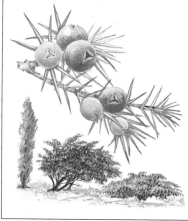

A shrub, 4 to 12 feet high (1.5 to 3.5 m) – though there is a prostrate form – with whorls of narrow evergreen leaves. Flowers, small, yellow, at the base of the leaves, appearing May to June. Fruit, a green, berry-like cone, appearing in June but not ripening until September or October of its second year, when it turns blue-black.

At the time of ripening, juniper berries are rich in oil, which is the source of their use as a flavouring. They are of course best known as the flavouring in gin, and most of the historical uses have been in one kind of drink or another. They have also been roasted and ground as a coffee substitute. In Sweden they are used to make a type of beer, and are often turned into jam. In France, 'genevrette' is made by fermenting a mixture of juniper berries and barley.

Small quantities of the ripe berries are probably best used for cooking with sauerkraut, or with white meat. But do experiment with drinks in which the berries have been steeped. Even gin is improved by, as it were, a double dose.

WALNUT
Juglans regia

Deciduous tree, with grey, fissured bark. Leaves are odd-pinnate, with 5 to 9 leaflets. Catkins followed by flowers. Nuts ripen in September.

The walnut was introduced to this country from Asia Minor four or five hundred years ago. It has rarely spread beyond those sites where it was planted and has consequently never been added to the British flora. Even these specimens have now been depleted because of the great popularity of walnut wood, particularly during the last century. But there are enough individual trees scattered around old woodland parks to make the nut worth a mention here.

Walnuts are best when they are fairly ripe and dry, in late October and November. Before this, the young 'wet' walnuts are rather taste-less. If you wish to pick them young, pick them in July whilst they are still green and make pickle from them. They should be soft enough to pass a knitting needle or skewer through. Prick them lightly with a fork to allow the pickle to permeate the skin, and leave them to stand in strong brine for about a week, until they are quite black. Drain and wash them and let them dry for two or three days more. Pack them into jars and cover them with hot pickling vinegar. Seal the jars and allow to stand for at least a month before eating.

HAZEL
Corylus avellana

Abundant throughout the British Isles, except in very damp areas. Grows in woods, hedgerows and scrubland. A shrub, 4 to 12 feet (1.5 to 3.5 m) high, with roundish, downy, toothed leaves. Best known for the yellow male catkins, called 'lambs' tails', which appear in the winter. Nuts from late August to October, ½ to 1 inch (1 to 2.5 cm) long, ovoid and encased in a thick green lobed husk.

Hazelnuts begin to ripen in mid-September, at about the same time that the leaves begin to yellow. Look for them at the edges of woods and in mature hedges. Search *inside* bushes for the nuts, as well as working round them, and scan them with the sun behind you if possible. Use a walking stick to bend down the branches, and gather the nuts into a basket that stays open whilst you are picking: a plastic bag with one handle looped over your picking wrist is a useful device.

If the ground cover under the bush is relatively clear or grass, then it is worthwhile giving the bush a shake. Some of the invisible ripe nuts should find their way on to the ground after this. In fact it is always worth searching the ground underneath a hazel. If there are nuts there which are dark or grey-brown in colour then the kernels will have turned to dust. But there is a chance that there will also be fresh windfalls that have not yet been picked on by birds.

Once you have gathered your nuts, keep them in a dry, warm place – but in their shells, so that the kernels don't dry out as well. You can use the nuts chopped or grated in salads, or with apple, raisins and raw oatmeal (muesli). Ground up in a blender, mixed with milk and chilled, they make a passable imitation of the Spanish drink *horchata* (properly made from the roots of the sedge *Cyperus esculentus*). But hazelnuts are such a rich food that it seems wasteful not to use them occasionally as a protein substitute. Weight for weight, they contain fifty per cent more protein, seven times more fat and five times more carbohydrate than hens' eggs. What better way of cashing in on such a meaty hoard than the unjustly infamous nut cutlet?

Mix two ozs (56 gm) of oil and two ozs of flour in a saucepan. Add a pint (568 ml) of stock and seasoning and stew for ten minutes, stirring all the time. Add three ozs (85 gm) of breadcrumbs and two ozs (56 gm) of grated hazelnuts. Cool the mixture and shape into cutlets. Dip the cutlets into an egg and milk mixture, coat with breadcrumbs and fry in oil until brown.

To make hazelnut bread, grind a cupful of young nuts, and mix with the same amount of self-raising flour, half a cup of sugar and a little salt. Beat an egg with milk, and add it to the mixture, beating, then kneading it until you have a stiff dough. Mould to a loaf shape, and bake in a medium oven for 50 minutes.

Hazel

BEECH
Fagus sylvatica

Widespread and common throughout the British Isles, especially on chalky soils. A stately tree, with smooth grey bark and leaves of a bright, translucent green. Nuts in September–October, four inside a prickly brown husk. When ripe this opens into four lobes, thus liberating the brown, three-sided nuts.

Beech

The botanical name *Fagus* originates from a Greek word meaning to eat, though in the case of the beech this is more likely to have referred to pigs than humans. This is not to say that beechmast – the usual term for the nuts – is disagreeable. Raw, or roasted and salted, it tastes not unlike young walnut. But the nuts are very small, and the collection and peeling of enough to make an acceptable meal is a tiresome business. This is also an obstacle to the rather more interesting use of beechmast as a source of vegetable oil. Although I have never tried the extraction process myself, mainly because of a lack of suitable equipment, it has been widely used on the Continent, particularly in times of economic hardship.

Although beech trees only fruit every three or four years, each tree produces a prodigious quantity of mast, and there is rarely any difficulty in finding enough. It should be gathered as early as possible, before the squirrels have taken it, and before it has had a chance to dry out. The three-faced nuts should be cleaned of any remaining husks, dirt or leaves and then ground, shells and all, in a small oil-mill. (For those with patience, a mincing machine or a strong blender should work as well.) The resulting pulp should be put inside a fine muslin bag and then in a press or under a heavy weight to extract the oil.

For those able to get this far, the results should be worthwhile. Every pound of nuts yields as much as three fluid ozs (85 ml) of oil. The oil itself is rich in fats and proteins, and provided it is stored in well-sealed containers, will keep fresh considerably longer than many other vegetable fats.

Beechnut oil can be used for salads or for frying, like any other cooking oil. Its most exotic application is probably beechnut butter, which is still made in some rural districts in the USA, and for which there was a patent issued in this country during the reign of George I.

In April the young leaves of the beech tree are almost translucent. They shine in the sun from the light passing through them. To touch they are silky, and tear like delicately thin rubber. It is difficult not to want to chew a few as you walk through a beech-wood in spring. And, fresh from the tree, they are indeed a fine salad vegetable, as sweet as a mild cabbage though much softer in texture.

An unusual way of utilising them is to make a potent liqueur, called beech leaf noyau. This probably originated in the Chilterns, where large plantations of beech were put down in the eighteenth and nineteenth centuries to service the chair-making trade.

Pack an earthenware or glass jar about nine-tenths full of young, clean leaves. Pour gin into the jar, pressing the leaves down all the time, until they are just covered. Leave to steep for about a fortnight. Then strain off the gin, which will by now have caught the brilliant green of the leaves. To every pint (568 ml) of gin add about three-quarters of a pound (350 gm) of sugar (more if you like your liqueurs very syrupy) dissolved in half a pint (284 ml) of boiling water, and a dash of brandy. Mix well and bottle as soon as cold.

The result is a thickish, sweet spirit, mild and slightly oily to taste, like *sake*, but devastating in its effects!

SWEET CHESTNUT
Castanea sativa

Well distributed throughout England, though scattered in Scotland. Fairly common in woods and parks. A tall,

> straight tree with single spear-shaped serrated leaves. Nuts
> in October and November, two or three carried in spherical
> green cases covered with long spines.

A nut to get your teeth into. And a harvest to get your hands into, if
the year is good and the nuts thick enough on the ground to warrant
a small sack rather than a basket. Although the tree was in all prob-
ability introduced to this country by the Romans, nothing seems
more English than gathering and roasting chestnuts on fine autumn
afternoons.

The best chestnut trees are the straight, old ones whose leaves
turn brown early. (Don't confuse them, by the way, with horse
chestnuts, whose inedible conkers look very similar to sweet chestnuts inside their spiny husks. In fact the trees are not related,
Castanea sativa being a cousin of the oak.) They will be covered with
the prickly fruit as early as September, and small specimens of the
nuts to come will be blown down early in the next month. Ignore
them, unless you can find some bright green ones which have just
fallen. They are undeveloped and will shrivel within a day or two.

The ripe nuts begin to fall late in October, and can be helped on
their way with a few judiciously thrown sticks. Opening the prickly
husks can be a painful business, and for the early part of the crop it is
as well to take a pair of gloves and some strong boots, the latter for
splitting the husks underfoot, the former for extricating the fruits.
The polished brown surface of the ripe nuts uncovered by the split
husk is positively alluring. You will want to stamp on every husk
you see, and rummage down through the leaves and spines to see if
the reward is glinting there.

Don't shy away from eating the nuts raw. If the stringy pith is
peeled away as well as the shell, most of their bitterness will go. But
roasting transforms them. They take on the sweetness and bulk of
some tropical fruit. As is the case with so much else in this book the
excitement lies as much in the rituals of preparation as in the food
itself. Chestnut roasting is an institution, rich with associations of
smell, and of welcomingly hot coals in cold streets. To do it efficiently at home, slit the skins, and put the nuts in the hot ash of an
open fire or close to the red coals – save one, which is put in uncut.
When this explodes, the others are ready. The explosion is fairly
ferocious, scattering hot shrapnel over the room, so sit well back
from the fire and make sure all the other nuts *have* been slit.

Chestnuts are a highly versatile vegetable. They can be pickled,
candied, or made into an amber with breadcrumbs and egg yolk.
Boiled with brussels sprouts they were Goethe's favourite dish.

Chopped, stewed and baked with red cabbage, they make a rich vegetable pudding.

Chestnut purée is an adaptable form in which to use the nuts. Shell and peel the chestnuts, and boil them in a thin stock for about forty minutes. Strain off the liquid and then rub the nuts through a sieve, or mash them in a liquidiser. The resulting purée can be seasoned and used as a substitute for potatoes, or form the basis of stuffings, soups and sweets.

A more elaborate way of storing the raw material of the nuts is to turn them into flour, as is done in some areas of the Mediterranean. You will need to collect a good number of young chestnuts and store them in a warm, dry and well-ventilated room for a couple of months. Then they must be individually shelled, and ground as finely as possible (a blender is the best way). The resulting yellowish flour is slightly fragrant and excellent in cakes and breads. But it can be reluctant to rise, and is probably best mixed half and half with ordinary wheat flour.

OAK
Quercus robur

An acorn-producing species common throughout Britain and Europe.

Acorns have been used as human food in times of famine, though like beechmast their chief economic use has been as animal fodder. The raw kernels are forbiddingly bitter to most palates, but chopped and roasted they can be used as a substitute for almonds.

In Europe the most common use of acorns has been in the roast form, as a substitute for coffee. They were recommended for this role during the war. The kernels were chopped, roasted to a light brown colour, ground up, and then roasted again.

LIME
Tilia europaea

Common in parks, by roadsides and in ornamental woods and copses. Flowers in July, a drooping cluster of heavily scented yellow blossoms. Leaves, large and heart-shaped, smooth above, paler below with a few tufts of fine white hairs. The lime is a tall tree when it is allowed to grow naturally, with a smooth, dark brown trunk usually interrupted by a few bosses.

The leaves are thick, cooling, and very glutinous. In high summer, before they begin to roughen, they make a sandwich filling in their own right, between thin slices of new bread, unsalted butter and just a sprinkling of lemon juice or Worcester sauce. Cut off the stalks and wash well, but otherwise put them between the bread as they come off the tree.

In late June and July the yellow flowers of mature lime trees have a delicious honey-like fragrance, and make one of the very best teas of all wild flowers. It is popular in France where it is sold under the name of *tilleul*.

The flowers should be gathered whilst they are in full bloom, and laid out on trays in a warm, well-ventilated room to dry. After two or three weeks they are ready for use. Make tea from them in the usual way, experimenting with strengths, and serve like China tea, without milk.

HAWTHORN
Crataegus monogyna

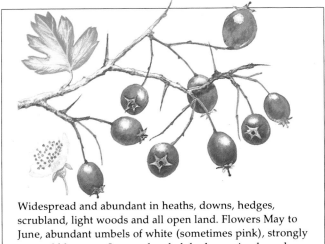

Widespread and abundant in heaths, downs, hedges, scrubland, light woods and all open land. Flowers May to June, abundant umbels of white (sometimes pink), strongly scented blossoms. Leaves deeply lobed on spiny branches. Whole shrub up to 20 feet (6 m) high.

The young April leaves – called bread and cheese by children – have a pleasantly nutty taste, and are a useful addition to spring salads. The buds can be picked much earlier in the year, though it takes an age to gather any quantity, and they tend to fall apart anyway. There is a splendid recipe for a spring pudding which makes use of the leaf buds; but I would save your energy for the eating, and use the larger and more plentiful young leaf shoots.

Make a light suet crust, well seasoned, and roll it out thinly and as long in shape as possible. Cover the surface with the young leaves, and push them slightly into the suet. Take some rashers of bacon, cut into fine strips and lay them across the leaves. Moisten the edges of the dough and roll it up tightly, sealing the edges as you go. Tie in a cloth and steam for at least an hour. Cut it in thick slices like a Swiss roll, and serve with gravy.

Alternatively, use the leaves in sandwiches, or in any of the recipes for wild spring greens. They also blend well with potatoes and almost any kind of nuts.

Haws are perhaps the most abundant berry of all in the autumn. Almost every hawthorn bush is festooned with small bunches of the round, dark-red berries, looking a little like spherical hips. They make a moderate jelly, but being a dry fruit need long simmering with a few crab apples to bring out all the juices and provide the necessary pectin. Otherwise the jelly will be sticky or rubbery. It is a good accompaniment to cream cheese.

MEDLAR
Mespilus germanica

Probably native, but occurring only very occasionally in hedgerows in the south, usually in gnarled, eccentric shapes produced by the wood's sensitivity to the wind. Fruit like a giant brown rose-hip, with the five-tailed calyx protruding from the head of the fruit like a crown.

The curious fact about the medlar is that its fruits need to be half-rotten – or 'bletted' – before they are edible. This seems to be a result of our climate not being warm enough to ripen the fruits, for in Mediterranean regions, where the tree is more widespread, the young fruit can be eaten straight off the tree. Here it stays rock-hard until mid-winter.

When the fruits are fully bletted, usually not before the November frosts, the brown flesh can be scraped out of the skin and eaten with cream and sugar. The fruits can also be baked whole, like apples, or made into jelly.

ROWAN, MOUNTAIN ASH
Sorbus aucuparia

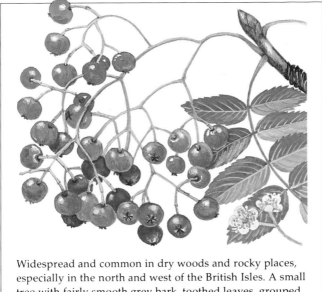

Widespread and common in dry woods and rocky places, especially in the north and west of the British Isles. A small tree with fairly smooth grey bark, toothed leaves, grouped in alternate pairs, and umbels of small white flowers. Fruit: large clusters of small orange berries, August to November.

The rowan is a favourite municipal tree, and is planted in great numbers along the edges of residential highways, but you should not have too much trouble in finding wild specimens. Their clusters of brilliant orange fruits are unmistakable in almost every setting, against grey limestone in the uplands, or the deep evergreen of scots pine on wintry heaths. Unless the birds have got there first, rowan berries can hang on the trees until January. They are best picked in October, when they have their full colour but have not yet become mushy.

You should cut the clusters whole from the trees, trim off any excess stalk, and then make a jelly in the usual way, with the addition of a little chopped crab apple to provide the pectin. (You should be able to find crabs growing not far away from your rowans.)

The jelly is a deliciously dark orange, with a sharp, marmaladish flavour, and is perfect with game and lamb.

HOP
Humulus lupulus

Locally frequent in hedges and damp thickets in England and Wales. Flowers July to August.

The green, cone-like female flowers of the hop have been used for flavouring beer since the ninth century. Yet though the plant is a British native, hops were not used for brewing in this country until the fifteenth century. Even then there was considerable opposition to their addition to the old ale recipes, and it was another hundred years before hop-growing became a commercial operation.

Wild hops can be used for home brewing, but a more intriguing and quite possibly older custom makes use of the very young shoots and leaves, picked not later than May. They may be an ancient wild vegetable, but most of the recipes came into being as a way of making frugal use of the mass of trimmings produced when the hop plantations were pruned in the spring.

The shoots can be chopped up and simmered in butter as a sauce, added to soups and omelettes, or, most popularly, cooked as asparagus. For the latter, strip the young shoots of the larger leaves, soak in salt water for an hour, drain and then plunge into boiling water for a few minutes until just tender. Serve with molten butter.

WILD SERVICE TREE
Sorbus torminalis

A relative of the rowan and the whitebeam. Largely confined to ancient woods and hedgerows on limestone soils in the west and stiff clays in the Midlands and south.

The wild service tree is one of the most local and retiring of our native trees, and knowledge of the fascinating history of its fruits has only recently been rediscovered.

The fruits, which appear in September, are round or pear-shaped and the size of small cherries. They are hard and bitter at first, but as autumn progresses they 'blet' and become very sweet. The taste is unlike anything else which grows wild in this country, with hints of damson, prune, apricot, sultana and tamarind.

Remains of the berries have been found in prehistoric sites and they must have been a boon before other sources of sugar were available. In areas where the tree was relatively widespread (e.g. the Weald of Kent) they continued to be a popular dessert fruit up to the beginning of this century. The fruits were gathered before they had bletted and strung up in clusters around a stick, which was hung up indoors, often by the hearth. They were picked off and eaten as they ripened, like sweets.

The berries were also used quite extensively in brewing. I have the house recipe of one Kentish pub that used to serve 'chequerberry beer':

'Pick off in bunches in October. Hang on a string like onions (look like swarm of bees). Hang till ripe. Cut off close to berries. Put them in stone or glass jars. Put sugar on – 1 lb to 5 lb of berries. Shake up well. Keep airtight until juice comes to the top. The longer kept the better. Can add brandy. Drink. Then eat berries!'

WHITEBEAM
Sorbus aria

Locally frequent in scrub and copses in the south of England, and popular as a suburban roadside tree. Also a very striking shrub, flashed with silver when the wind turns up the pale undersides of the leaves.

The bunched red berries are edible as soon as they begin to 'blet' – or go rotten, like service berries. John Evelyn recommended them in a concoction with new wine and honey, though they are rather disappointing.

Whitebeam

WILD CHERRY
Prunus avium

Widespread and frequent in hedgerows and woods, especially beech. A lofty tree with shining, reddish-brown bark and an abundance of white flowers in the spring. The fruit is like a small, dark-red, cultivated cherry.

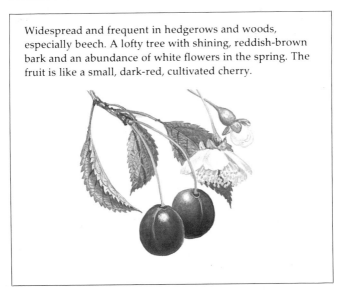

The fruit of the wild cherry can be either sweet or bitter. It used to be sold occasionally in London on the branch.

SLOE, BLACKTHORN
Prunus spinosa

Widespread and abundant in woods and hedgerows throughout the British Isles, though thinning out in the north of Scotland. A stiff, dense shrub, up to 12 feet (3.5 m) high, with long thorns and oval leaves. The flowers are small and pure white and appear before the leaves. Fruit: a small, round, very dark-blue berry covered when young with a paler bloom.

The sloe is the ancestor of all our cultivated plums. Crossed with the cherry-plum (*Prunus cerasifera*), selected, crossed again, it eventually produced fruits as sweet and sumptuous as the Victoria. Yet the wild sloe is the tartest, most acid berry you will ever taste. Just one cautious bite into the green flesh will make the whole of the inside of your mouth creep. But a barrowload of sloe-stones were collected during the excavation of a Neolithic lake village at Glastonbury. Were they just used for dyeing? Or did our ancestors have hardier palates than us?

For all its potent acidity, the sloe is very far from being a useless fruit. It makes a clear, sprightly jelly, and that most agreeable of liqueurs, sloe gin.

The best time to pick sloes for this drink is immediately after the first frost, which makes the skins softer and more permeable. Sloe gin made at this time will, providentially, just be ready in time for Christmas. Pick about a pound of the marble-sized berries (you will probably need a glove as the spines are stiff and sharp). If they have not been through a frost, pierce the skin of each one with a skewer, to help the gin and the juices get together more easily. Mix the sloes with half their weight of sugar, and half fill the bottles with this mixture. Pour gin into the bottles until they are nearly full, and seal tightly. Store for at least two months, and shake occasionally to help dissolve and disperse the sugar. The result is a brilliant, deep pink liqueur, sour-sweet and refreshing to taste, and demonstrably potent. Don't forget to eat the berries from the bottle, which will have quite lost their bitter edge, and soaked up a fair amount of the gin themselves. As an alternative, try replacing the gin in the recipe above with brandy or aquavit.

BULLACE, DAMSONS AND WILD PLUMS
Prunus species

The true bullace *Prunus domestica* ssp. *insititia* may be a scarce native of old hedgerows, but the majority of wild plums found in the countryside are either seeded from garden trees, or are reverted orchard specimens. Fruit blue-black, brownish, or green-yellow, and usually midway in size between a sloe and a cultivated damson.

Wild plums are ripe from early October, and, unlike sloes, are usually just about sweet enough to eat raw. Otherwise they can be used like sloes, in jellies, gin, and autumn puddings (see p. 81).

Wild plums make excellent dark jams, and the French jam specialist Gisèle Tronche has pointed out how the addition of a little ground cumin seed and aniseed can improve conventional recipes. Alternatively try her late autumn, wild fruit 'humeur noir', which she describes as having 'the colour of a good, healthy, black-tempered funk'.

Macerate 2 lbs (900 gm) of stoned dark damsons with ½ lb (225 gm) sugar overnight. Boil together ½ lb (225 gm) of elderberries and 1½ lbs (675 gm) of blackberries for ten minutes. Add the plums, 1½ lbs (675 gm) of sugar, a tablespoon of cider vinegar and the juice of one lemon, and bring to the boil again. Cook for about an hour, until the desired consistency is reached.

Bullace

JUNE BERRY
Amelanchier intermedia

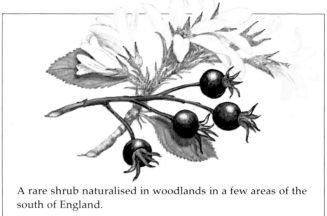

A rare shrub naturalised in woodlands in a few areas of the south of England.

The purplish-red berries are sweet to taste, and can be eaten uncooked, or made into pies. In America they are sometimes canned for winter use.

ELDER
Sambucus nigra

Widespread and common in woods, hedgerows and waste
places. Flowers June to July. A tall, fast-growing shrub,
with a corky bark, white pith in the heart of the branches,
and a scaly surface to the young twigs. Leaves usually in
groups of five; large, dark-green and slightly toothed.
Flowers: umbels of numerous tiny cream-white flowers.
Fruits: August to October, clusters of small, reddish-black
berries.

To see the mangy, decaying skeletons of elders in the winter you
would not think the bush was any use to man or beast. Nor would
the acrid stench of the young leaves in spring change your opinion.
But by the end of June the whole shrub is covered with great sprays
of sweet-smelling flowers, for which there are probably more uses
than any other single species of blossom. Even in orthodox medicine they have an acknowledged role as an ingredient in skin oint-
ments and eye-lotions.

Elder flowers can be munched straight off the branch on a hot
summer's day, and taste as frothy as a glass of ice-cream soda. Something even closer to that drink can be made by putting a bunch of
elder flowers in a jug with boiling water, straining the liquid off
when cool, and sweetening.

Cut the elder flower clusters whole, with about two inches (5 cm)
of stem attached to them. (This is needed for one of the recipes.)

Always check that they are free of insects, and discard any that are badly infested. The odd grub or two can be removed by hand. But never wash the flowers as this will remove much of the fragrance. The young buds can be pickled or added to salads. The flowers themselves, separated from the stalks, make what is indisputably the best sparkling wine besides champagne. But the two most famous recipes for elder flowers are the preserve they make with gooseberries and elder-flower fritters.

To make the preserve, trim off as much of the rather bitter stalk as you can, and have ready four flower heads for each pound of gooseberries. Top, tail and wash the gooseberries in the usual way, and put them into a pan with one pint (560 ml) of water for every pound (450 gm) of fruit. Simmer for half an hour, mashing the fruit to a pulp as you do. Add one pound of sugar for each pound of fruit, stir rapidly until dissolved, and bring to the boil. Then add the elder flowers, tied in muslin, and boil rapidly until the setting point is reached. Remove the flowers and pot in the usual way. (See p. 20 for a few extra notes on jams generally.) The flavour is quite transformed from that of plain gooseberry jam, and reminiscent of muscat grapes. It is good with ice-cream and other sweets.

The fritters are made with a thin batter prepared from 4 tablespoons of flour, one egg and about 1½ cupfuls of water. Hold the flower heads by the stalks and dip into the batter. Strain off any excess, and then plunge into hot oil and deep-fry until golden brown. Trim off the excess stalk and serve with sugar and perhaps a little fresh mint. They make a perfect and delicately flavoured finish to a summer meal.

The fruits are useful as additions to a number of cooked recipes in which any unpleasant aftertaste completely disappears.

The berries are ripe when the clusters begin to turn upside down. Gather the clusters whole by cutting them from the stems, picking only those where the very juicy berries have not started to wrinkle or melt. Wash them well, and strip them from the stalks with a fork. They are good added whole to apple pies, or added as a makeweight to blackberry jelly. (Both berries are on the bush at the same time, so if you are making this they can be gathered straight into the same basket.)

My favourite elderberry recipe is for Pontack Sauce, a relic from those days when every retired military gentleman carried his patent sauce as an indispensable part of his luggage.

There are any number of variants of Pontack Sauce, particularly from the hunting country in the Midlands. This one from Leicestershire probably used claret instead of vinegar in the original (Pontack's was owned by Château Haut Brion).

Pour one pint (568 ml) of boiling vinegar (or claret) over one pint of elderberries in a stone jar or casserole dish. Cover, and allow the jar to stand overnight in an oven at very low heat. Next day pour off the liquid, put it in a saucepan with a teaspoon of salt, a blade of mace, 40 peppercorns, 12 cloves, a finely chopped onion and a little ginger. Boil for ten minutes and then bottle securely with the spices.

The sauce was reputedly meant to be kept for seven years before use. My patience ran out after seven days, but having made rather a large bottle, I can report a distinct improvement in richness after the first few years! It has a fine fruity taste, a little like a thick punch, and is especially good with liver.

FLOWERING PLANTS

SWEET GALE, BOG MYRTLE
Myrica gale

Locally common in bogs, marshes and wet heaths, mainly in Scotland, Ireland, north Wales and the south-west of England. Flowers April to May. A deciduous shrub, 2 to 4 feet (60 to 120 cm) high with red and orange (female and male) catkins on separate plants. These flowers appear before the leaves, which are grey-green, narrow, toothed, on shiny reddish twigs.

Gale was traditionally used for the flavouring of beer before hops were taken into service to this country. There is evidence that this drink was being brewed in Anglo-Saxon times, and the isolated patches of sweet gale which grow around old monasteries and other early settlements suggest that it was occasionally taken into cultivation, outside its natural habitats.

The brewing recipe is rather elaborate, so experiment with sweet gale as a herb, and use it to flavour existing drinks. Its warm aroma – with hints of balsam, cloves and pine resin – will give a retsina-like tang to wine. The leaves are also good as a stuffing for roast chicken.

STINGING NETTLE
Urtica dioica

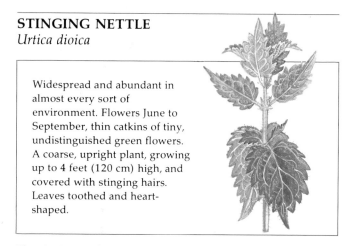

Widespread and abundant in almost every sort of environment. Flowers June to September, thin catkins of tiny, undistinguished green flowers. A coarse, upright plant, growing up to 4 feet (120 cm) high, and covered with stinging hairs. Leaves toothed and heart-shaped.

The stinging nettle is one of the commonest of all edible wild plants, and one of the most useful. There is evidence that nettles were cultivated in eighteenth-century Scandinavia, the coarse fibres of the stalks being used for cloth as well as the leaves for food. Samuel Pepys enjoyed a nettle 'porridge' on 25 February 1661, though he gives no details of the dish. Scott has the old gardener in *Rob Roy* raising nettles under glass as 'early spring kail'. And in the Second World War hundreds of tons were gathered annually in Great Britain for the extraction of chlorophyll and of dyes for camouflage nets.

Nettles should not be picked for eating after the beginning of June. In high summer the leaves become coarse in texture, unpleasantly bitter in taste and decidedly laxative. The best time of all for them is when the young shoots are no more than a few inches high. Pick these shoots whole, or, if you are gathering later in the year, just the tops and the young pale green leaves. It is as well to use gloves whilst doing this, even if you do have a Spartan belief in the protection of the firm grasp.

Before cooking your nettles remove the tougher stems and wash well. They can be used in a number of ways. As a straight vegetable they should be boiled gently in a closed pan for about four minutes, in no more water than adheres to the leaves after washing. Strain off the water well, add a large knob of butter and plenty of seasoning (and perhaps some chopped onion), and simmer for a further five minutes, turning and mashing all the while. The resulting purée is interestingly fluffy in texture, but rather insipid to taste, and for my money nettles are better used as additions to other dishes than as vegetables in their own right.

Nettle soup is one such dish. Boil the nettles as above, and press through a fine sieve or reduce to a purée in a blender. Melt an ounce (30 gm) of butter in a pan and stir in an ounce of flour and salt and pepper. Remove from the stove and beat in a pint (568 ml) of hot milk gradually till the mixture is quite smooth. Boil up this sauce and simmer for five minutes, stirring all the time. Then pour on to the nettle purée and mix thoroughly. Prepare some fried bread in bacon fat, and add to the soup before serving.

Another splendid recipe is for nettle haggis. The nettle purée is mixed with leeks and cabbage, freshly fried bacon and partially cooked oatmeal (or rice or barley), the whole boiled for an hour or so in a muslin bag, and served with gravy.

Young nettle leaves have also been made into beer and used as the basis for a herbal tea.

BISTORT
Polygonum bistorta

> Widespread and locally common in wet, hilly pastures throughout the British Isles, except the south. Flowers June to August, pink spikes topping off a straight, hairless stem about 2 feet (60 cm) high. Leaves: triangular or arrow-shaped on long stalks.

In the early spring of 1971 the following advertisement appeared in the Personal Column of *The Times*: 'Polygonum bistorta – How is your Dock Pudding?' The copy invited entrants for the first World Championship Dock Pudding Contest, to be held in the Calder Valley in Yorkshire. Evidently the tradition of eating bistort was far from dead in the north, for there were over fifty competitors from this one valley alone.

Bistort is a plant of damp upland meadows, out of the range of nibbling sheep (though one Calder Valley man claimed that the best plants grew on his grandad's grave on Sowerby Top). It usually appears as a basic ingredient of Easter Ledger, or Easter Herb, Pudding. The bulk of the popular local names refer to the plant's function in this pudding, from Passion Dock (from Passion-tide, the last two weeks of Lent, which was the proper time for eating this rather scant dish) to Easter Giant, a contraction of Easter Mangiant (from the French *manger*, to eat).

There is an enormous variety of different recipes for the Ledger Pudding, most of them originating in the Lake District. This one is from Westmorland:

Take a good bagful of spring leaves, mainly bistort, but also young nettle tops, dandelion leaves, lady's mantle, etc. Wash them well and put into a little boiling water for ten minutes. Strain and chop the leaves. Add one beaten egg, one hard-boiled egg chopped small, butter, salt and pepper, and mix well into the leaves. Put back in the saucepan, heat through, and then transfer to a hot pudding basin to shape.

Bistort   Red Leg

RED LEG
Polygonum persicaria

Widespread and common throughout the British Isles in
damp, shady places, near ditches, etc. Flowers June to
October.

Leaves are rather insipid, but they can be used in mixed greens, or in
the Easter Pudding mix (above).

COMMON SORREL
Rumex acetosa

Widespread and common in
grassland and heathy places,
especially on acid soils,
throughout the British Isles.
Flowers May to August,
spikes of small red and green
flowers on a smooth stem 6
inches to 2 feet (15 to 60 cm)
high. Leaves arrow-shaped
and clasping the stem near
the top of the plant.

Sorrel is one of the very first green plants to appear in the spring.
The leaves can often be picked as early as February when other
greenstuffs are scarce. They are marvellously cool and sharp when
raw, like young plum skins, but perhaps too acid for some palates.

In Gerard's time the leaves were boiled and eaten, or made into a
green sauce for fish. For this they were pulped raw and mixed with
sugar and vinegar. Dorothy Hartley describes a late seventeenth-

century recipe for the sauce, in which bread, apple, sugar and vinegar are boiled together until soft, then mixed, still hot, with sorrel purée. The mixture is then strained, yielding a thick green juice with a strong pungent taste.

In France sorrel is used in an enormous variety of dishes. The chopped leaves are added to give a sharp flavour to the heavy soups of potato, lentil and haricot bean. The cooked purée is added to omelettes, or, like the sauce, served as an accompaniment to veal or fish dishes.

To make a rich sorrel soup, chop a pound (450 gm) of the leaves with a large onion and a sprig of rosemary. Mix well with one tablespoon of flour and simmer the mixture in 3 ozs (85 gm) of butter for about ten minutes, stirring well all the time. Add two quarts (just over 2 litres) of boiling water, two tablespoons of breadcrumbs and seasoning. Simmer for one hour. When ready, take off the boil and just before serving stir in a well-beaten mixture of two egg yolks and ¼ pint (142 ml) of cream.

In parts of the north and the Midlands, sorrel was used as a substitute for apple in tarts and turnovers, during the fruit off-season between the last apples in March and the first gooseberries. Sorrel's plum-skin sharpness can make it an interesting stand-in for fruit in other dishes.

CURLED DOCK
Rumex crispus

> The most widespread of all our docks, growing as happily in seaside shingle as in suburban field edges.

The crinkly leaves, which can grow up to a foot (30 cm) long, are bitter, but have been used as a vegetable in the United States. The leaves are gathered very young and cooked with bacon or ham and a little vinegar. The leaves of our commonest dock, the broad-leaved dock (*Rumex obtusifolia*), have been used in the same way, though they are even more bitter.

Parents can pick a leaf or two of dock and crumple them up to rub into the skin of a small child who has been stung by a nettle. The miraculous alleviation of the pain is probably entirely psychological; but the confidence-trick is as valuable as the notions of tooth-fairies and Father Christmas, and should be perpetuated stoutly.

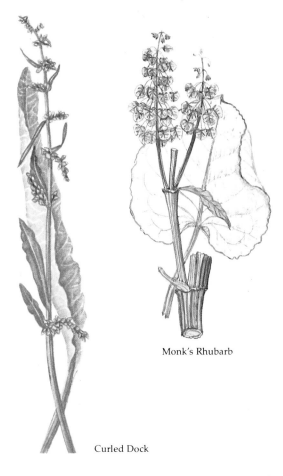

Monk's Rhubarb

Curled Dock

MONK'S RHUBARB
Rumex alpinus

An uncommon species of dock, with large heart-shaped
leaves.

Monk's rhubarb was introduced as a pot-herb in the Middle Ages,
and in the parts of Scotland and the north of England where it still
grows, it is rarely found far from houses.

HOTTENTOT FIG
Caprobrotus edulis

Trailing branched perennial with fleshy leaves. Yellow, pink or magenta flowers with yellow stamens. Fleshy fruit appears May to July. Found on cliffs, particularly in Devon and Cornwall; originally native to south Africa.

Its fruits, the figs, are edible but rather tangy.

SEA PURSLANE
Halimione portulacoides

Common on saltmarshes in the south and east of England. Flowers July to October.

The oval, fleshy leaves of this maritime plant make a succulent addition to salads. They can also be stir-fried with fish or meat.

Sea Purslane

Fat-hen

FAT-HEN
Chenopodium album

Common in cultivated and waste ground throughout British Isles. Flowers June to September. An undistinguished plant, up to 3 feet (90 cm) tall, with stiff upright stems and diamond-shaped leaves. Flowers: pale green, minute and bunched into spikes.

Fat-hen is one of those plants that thrive in the company of humans. Prepare a manure heap in your garden and fat-hen will in all likelihood begin to grow there within a few months. It is one of the very first plants to colonise ground that has been disturbed by roadworks or housebuilding, its stiff, mealy spikes often appearing in prodigious quantity. No wonder that its use as a food plant dates back to prehistoric times. Remains of the plant have been found in Neolithic settlements all over Europe. The seeds also formed part of the last, ritual gruel fed to Tollund Man (the man whose perfectly preserved corpse, stomach contents included, was recovered from a bog in Denmark in 1950).

In Anglo-Saxon times the plant was apparently of sufficient importance to have villages named after it. As *melde* it gave its name to Melbourn in Cambridgeshire, and Milden in Suffolk. The introduction of spinach largely put an end to the use of the plant, but its leaves continued to be eaten in Ireland and the Scottish islands for a long while, and in many parts of Europe during the famine conditions of the last war. It has recently transpired that early people were lucky in this fortuitous choice of a staple vegetable: it contains more iron and protein than either cabbage or spinach, and more Vitamin B1 and calcium than raw cabbage.

It should be prepared and cooked in the same way as spinach, as a green vegetable, or in soups.

GOOD KING HENRY
Chenopodium bonus-henricus

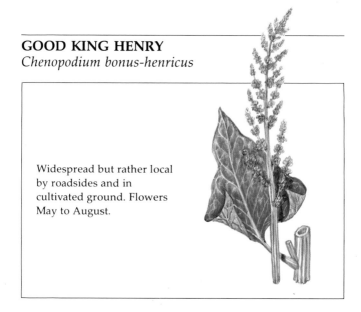

Widespread but rather local by roadsides and in cultivated ground. Flowers May to August.

Another food plant of great antiquity, the remains of which have been found in Neolithic encampments. In medieval and Elizabethan times it was occasionally taken into cultivation, and this practice has recently been revived.

The young shoots can also be cooked as asparagus, if they are picked in the spring when they are not more than 8 inches (20 cm) high.

COMMON ORACHE
Atriplex patula

Widespread and abundant throughout the British Isles, in bare and waste ground. Flowers July to September.

Young leaves and shoots may be used as a substitute for spinach.

Common Orache

SPEAR-LEAVED ORACHE
Atriplex hastata

Frequent throughout the British Isles, especially near the sea. Flowers July to September.

Use as common orache on previous page.

PIGWEED
Amaranthus retroflexus

A curious casual of waste and cultivated ground, with dense spikes of dry, greenish flowers.

The plant originated in tropical America and was much used by the Indians. The leaves, boiled, made a mild green vegetable, and the black seeds were ground into flour.

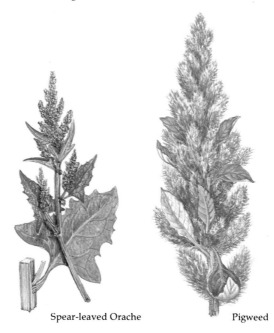

Spear-leaved Orache   Pigweed

MARSH SAMPHIRE, GLASSWORT
Salicornia species

Common and plentiful on saltmarshes round most British coasts. Flowers August to September. Glassworts are highly succulent plants and vary from single unbranched stems to thick stubbly bushes up to 1 foot (25 cm) tall. The stems are plump, shiny and jointed. Flowers minute, and only really visible as one or two white to red stamens growing out of the junctions in the stems.

Samphire has a liking for muddy situations, and grows in such abundance on some saltmarshes that a communal forage is the most sensible and agreeable way to harvest it. You go out at low tide, with buckets and wellingtons, through the sea-aster and wormwood in the rough ground at the edge of the saltings, on to the tidal reaches where the crop grows. This is a world criss-crossed by deep and hidden creeks, by which you will be tripped, cut off and plastered up to the thigh with glistening wet mud. In these creeks the samphire grows tall and bushy, like an amiable desert cactus.

On the poorer, sandier flats the size of the plants is less distinctive and they tend to grow as single shoots not more than 6 inches (15 cm) high. Yet they make up for this in sheer numbers. Often a bed can completely carpet several acres of marsh, and look as though it could be cut with a lawnmower.

When you have found your patch there is no way of escaping half an hour in a stooping position to do the picking. There are those who have tried to cut and lift the shoots with shears, but samphire is a wily plant, and cut like this will just flop over into the mud. Hunched up and grubbing about in the mud is the only way to appreciate the flavour of samphire-gathering.

There are two ways of actually picking the plant. Early in the season, whilst the shoots are still thin and tender, they should be pinched off above the root. Later in the year, when most of the growth has finished and the plants have developed a tough fibrous core, the whole plant can be pulled up. There are slightly different ways of cooking the young shoots and the whole plant.

When you have got your samphire home, wash it well and remove the pieces of seaweed that will inevitably be stuck to some of the plants. But never leave samphire to stand in water for more than a few hours. In stagnant water it quickly begins to decay. If you wish to keep it for a day or two before eating, choose a dry place open to the air.

The very young shoots, picked in June or July, make a crisp and tangy salad vegetable. Try chewing some sprigs straight from the marsh. They are very refreshing in spite of their slightly salty taste. To cook them, boil in a little water for about ten minutes, drain and simmer with a knob of butter. They go very well with poultry and lamb.

The whole plants picked in August and September are best served as an asparagus-like starter. Leave the roots on and simmer the plants upside-down in a saucepan of water for not more than 10 minutes. Drain, and serve whole in a bowl, with molten butter. (Samphire plants, being rather low in weight, cool off quickly, so it is as well to melt the butter first before pouring it on to the vegetable.) Eat by holding the roots and sliding the stems between the teeth, to draw the flesh off the tough central spine.

Another way of using samphire is to pickle it. This was once done by filling jars with the chopped shoots, covering with spiced vinegar, and placing in a baker's oven as it cooled off over the weekend. I would imagine that the result of 48 hours' simmering would be on the sloppy side, to say the least. To maintain the crisp texture of the plant and at least some of its brilliant green colour it is best to do no more than put it under cold pickling vinegar.

Finally, for a culinary pun, cook equal quantities of samphire and spaghetti, and serve together as a kind of *paglia e fieno*, the Italian green and white noodle dish.

SEA BEET, WILD SPINACH
Beta vulgaris

Common on banks and shingle by the sea, except in Scotland. Flowers June to September, tiny green blossoms in long leafy spikes. Grows up to 3 feet (90 cm) high with shiny, fleshy leaves.

Sea Beet

One of the happy exceptions to the small-leaved tendency among wild vegetables. Some of the bottom leaves of the sea beet can grow as large and as heavy as those of any cultivated spinach, and creak like parchment when you touch them.

You will be able to pick the leaves between April and October – big, fleshy ones from the base of the plant and thinner, spear-shaped ones near the head. Try and strip the larger leaves from their central spine as you pick them; it will save much time during preparation for cooking.

Always take special care in washing wild spinach leaves. The bushy clumps they grow in are often the only prominent vegetation along coastal paths and sea walls, and can be targets for perambulating dogs. Remove also the miscellaneous herbage you will inevitably have grubbed up whilst picking the leaves, and the more substantial stems.

Wild spinach can be used in identical ways to the garden variety. The small leaves which grow on specimens very close to the sea are often as much as a sixteenth of an inch (1.5 mm) thick, and are ideal for salads. The larger ones should be boiled briskly in a large saucepan with not more than half an inch (1 to 2 cm) of water. Leave the lid on for a few minutes, and at intervals chop and press down the leaves. When the vegetable has changed colour to a very dark green, remove the lid altogether and simmer for a further two or three minutes. Then transfer the spinach to a colander, and press out as much liquid as possible (saving it for gravies, stock, etc.). Return the greens to the saucepan, and toss over a low heat with a knob of butter. The taste is a good deal tangier than cultivated spinach, and good additions are diced tomatoes and grated nuts.

The most intriguing recipe I know for spinach is for a seventeenth-century spinach tart. Boil up the spinach in the usual way, and chop it up with a few hard-boiled egg yolks. Set into a pastry tart case, and pour on a sauce made of melted sugar, raisins and a touch of cinnamon. Bake in a moderate oven for about half an hour.

CHICKWEED
Stellaria media

 Widespread and abundant throughout the British Isles in gardens and disturbed ground. Flowers throughout the year, a tiny, white, star-like flower, with five deeply divided petals. A weak plant which tends to straggle and creep before it has reached any height. It has single lines of fine hairs up alternate sides of the stem. Leaves: bright green and soft.

Chickweed is generally regarded as a bane in gardens. Yet it is one of the most deliciously tender of all wild vegetables. Gerard prescribed it for 'little birdes in cadges . . . when they loath their meate'. But even in his time it was cooked as a green vegetable, and later hawked around city streets by itinerant vegetable sellers.

Next time you are weeding, try saving the chickweed instead of composting it. Those without gardens should be able to find some by any field edge, even in the winter months. The leaves are too small to be picked individually, so strip bunches of the whole plant; the stems are just as tender to eat as the leaves. (But avoid confusion with the stiff, hairy, mouse-ear chickweed, and the smooth, upright, red-stemmed petty spurge, which has a slight superficial resemblance to *Stellaria media*.)

Wash the sprigs well, and put into a saucepan without any additional water. Add a knob of butter or a spoonful of oil, seasoning, and some chopped spring onions. Simmer gently for about four to five minutes, turning all the time. Finish off with a dash of lemon juice or a sprinkling of grated nutmeg.

Chickweed is one of the earliest wild vegetables to come into leaf, and it is a good base for winter, or early spring, salads. Try mixing the young shoots with equal quantities of dandelion leaves, garlic mustard, hairy bittercress (for a hint of pepperiness) and charlock (for bulk). Dress with a light, sharp salad dressing made from sunflower oil and lemon juice.

BLADDER CAMPION
Silene vulgaris

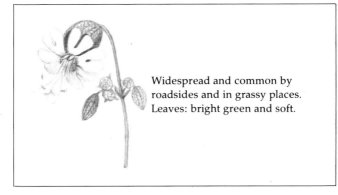

Widespread and common by roadsides and in grassy places. Leaves: bright green and soft.

The young shoots and leaves can be used like chickweed, and added to spring salads or cooked as greens.

OREGON GRAPE
Mahonia aquifolium

A member of the barberry family, naturalised in a number of places in open woodland and game coverts. An ever-green shrub, up to four feet (120 cm) high. The dark, white-bloomed berries form in bunches like miniature grapes.

They can be eaten raw, though they are rather acid, and are best made into a jelly.

CORN POPPY, FIELD POPPY
Papaver rhoeas

Widespread and abundant in arable fields and by roadsides. Becomes scarcer in Wales, north-west England and northern Scotland. Flowers June to October, deep scarlet, floppy petals at the top of a thin, hairy stalk, 1 to 2 feet (30 to 60 cm) high. The seed-pods are hairless, and flat-topped like an inverted cone.

It was once believed that smelling poppies gave you a headache, that staring at them for too long made you go blind. Superstitions about the supposed poisonousness of the flower still persist, notably the belief that the seed heads contain opium. In fact no parts of the common field poppy are narcotic, least of all the dry seeds. It is *Papaverum somniferum* from which opium is derived by the cutting and tapping of the juice from the unripe seed heads. Yet the dry ripe seeds of the opium poppy are entirely edible, and indeed are the poppy seeds of commerce, used extensively in baking. Corn poppy seeds make an acceptable, though less flavoursome, substitute.

The seed heads start to dry in September, and are ready for picking when they are grey-brown in colour, and have a number of small holes just below the edge of the flat top. (These are vents through which the seeds normally escape.) The seed in ripe heads can be readily shaken out of these holes.

Pick a handful of these heads, and put them straight into a paper bag. Remove the seeds by inverting the heads and shaking them into the bag. Any that cling on to their contents are not really ripe.

Poppy seeds are slate grey in colour and have an elusive taste. They are extensively used in European and Middle Eastern cookery, particularly for sprinkling on bread, rolls, cakes and biscuits. But they also go well with honey as a dressing for fruit, and with noodles and macaroni.

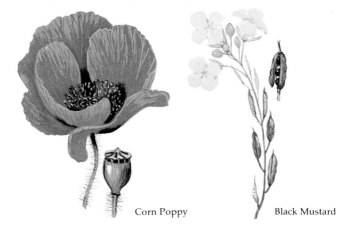

Corn Poppy   Black Mustard

BLACK MUSTARD
Brassica nigra

Quite common as an escape from cultivation on waysides and waste places.

Use the young leaves as tangy additions to spring salads and cooked greens.

Black mustard's seeds begin to ripen in August to September. You are unlikely to be able to gather more than a pinch, but try pressing them into the cheese on the top of Welsh rarebits before cooking.

WILD CABBAGE
Brassica oleracea

A scarce plant of the sea cliffs, probably the ancestor of all our garden cabbages. Today the plant is rare in its natural habitat. Yet escaped garden *Brassicas* sometimes revert to this form if they are allowed to go to seed. Flowering stems up to 4 feet (120 cm) high. Flowers yellow, May to August, appearing in long clusters.

You can tell them easily from the mustards and other related plants by their thick, greyish, fleshy leaves. They are bitter raw, but after long simmering are acceptable to eat.

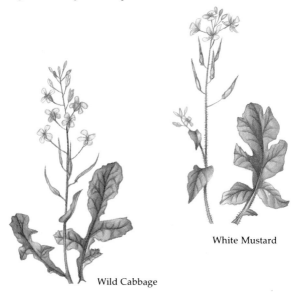

White Mustard

Wild Cabbage

WHITE MUSTARD
Sinapis alba

A common weed in arable land, and an escape from
cultivation, especially on chalky soils. Flowers May to
October. This is the mustard of 'mustard and cress'.

Under cultivation the plants are picked when they are only a few
inches high. In the wild they need to be picked rather later for certain identification, by which time they tend to be slightly bitter.

Use as chickweed in spring salads or in cooked greens.

SEA KALE
Crambe maritima

Widespread but extremely
local on sand and shingle
near the sea. Flowers June to
August. A cabbage-like plant,
growing in large clumps with
huge grey-green leaves, very
fleshy and glaucous. The
flowers are white and four-
petalled, and grow in a broad
cluster.

In many areas on the south coast villagers would watch for the
shoots to appear, pile sand and shingle round them to blanch out
the bitterness and cut them in the summer to take to the markets in
the nearest big town.

Up to the 19th century sea kale was a relatively common plant
around the coasts. But in 1799, the botanist William Curtis wrote a
pamphlet called *Directions for the culture of the Crambe Maritima or Sea
Kale, for the use of the Table*. As a result the vegetable was taken up by

Covent Garden, and demand for the naturally growing shoots increased greatly. This intensive collection was to have the effect of substantially reducing the population of wild sea kale. So be sparing if you do pick it, and do not take more than two or three stems from each plant. Use young shoots or the lower parts of the leaf stalks, particularly any that you can find which have been growing under the ground. (They sometimes push their way through up to 3 feet (90 cm) of shingle, and when harvesting you will need a sharp knife to cut through the thick stems.)

To cook the sea kale, cut the stems into manageable lengths and boil in salted water until tender (about 20 minutes). Then serve and eat with melted butter, like asparagus. Alternatively, use lemon juice or sauce hollandaise. The very young shoots and leaves can also be eaten raw as a salad.

COMMON SCURVY-GRASS
Cochlearia officinalis

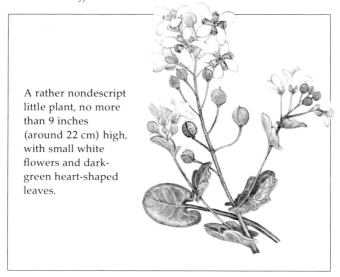

A rather nondescript little plant, no more than 9 inches (around 22 cm) high, with small white flowers and dark-green heart-shaped leaves.

Once famous as the major source of Vitamin C on long sea voyages. It was taken on board in the form of dried bundles or distilled extracts. But it is an unpleasantly bitter plant, and the taste was often disguised with spices.

But sailors were not the only ones with reason to fear scurvy, and fads for early morning scurvy-grass drinks and scurvy-grass sandwiches abounded right up till the middle of the nineteenth century. It was only the ready availability of citrus fruits which finally made the plant obsolete.

Scurvy-grass still grows abundantly round cliffs and banks near the sea, and it was probably its convenient proximity that made it the favourite maritime anti-scorbutic.

HORSERADISH
Armoracia rusticana

Common in waste ground in England and Wales; rare in Scotland and Ireland. Flowers from May to September, a shock of white blossoms on a long spike. Leaves: large, slightly toothed, and dock-like, growing straight up from the root stem to a height of about 3 feet (90 cm).

There can scarcely be any other plant of such wide commercial use that is so neglected in the wild. Small jars of horseradish sauce sell for 80p, yet the plant grows untouched and in abundance on waste ground throughout England.

The rougher the ground, the more horseradish seems to relish it. It will grow on derelict gardens, bomb sites, even abandoned brick piles. So you should have no trouble in finding a patch where you can obtain permission to dig up the roots.

There can be no mistaking its crinkly, palm-like leaves, but if you are in any doubt, crush them between your fingers: they should have the characteristic horseradish smell. A spade – desirable when gathering all roots – is imperative with horseradish. The plant is a perennial, and carries an extensive and complex root-system. You will need to dig quite deep and chop the woody structure to obtain a section for use.

The worst part of preparing horseradish is the peeling. Any section will be intractably knobbly, and need considerable geometric skill before it can be reduced to a manageable shape. Once it has been, the remains of the brown outer layer should be pared off with a sharp knife.

You will be left with some pure white chunks of horseradish which need to be grated before then can be used. This is best done out of doors, as the fumes put the most blinding onions to shame.

The freshly-grated root can be used as it stands, as a garnish for roast beef. But use it fairly quickly, as it loses its potency in a few days. To make an instant sauce from it, whip it up with some plain yoghourt and a little sugar and seasoning. A more substantial and longer-lasting sauce is made by mixing a teaspoon of dry mustard with a tablespoon of cold water, and blending until smooth. Combine with six heaped tablespoons of grated horseradish and salt and pepper. Allow to stand for a quarter of an hour. Then blend into a cupful of white sauce.

HAIRY BITTERCRESS
Cardamine hirsuta

Common and widespread in gardens and other bare, waste places. Flowers from March to September, but the leaves can be picked most months of the year.

A pleasantly tangy plant, sweeter than watercress.

CUCKOO FLOWER, LADY'S SMOCK
Cardamine pratensis

Common in damp
meadows, woods
and by the edges of
streams. Flowers
April to June.

The leaves are slightly hot, and have been used as an ingredient of
Easter Pudding (p. 48).

SHEPHERD'S PURSE
Capsella bursa-pastoris

Abundant and widespread in waste
and cultivated places. Flowers
throughout the year.

Slightly peppery in taste. Popular in China, where it is stir-fried, like
cabbage.

WINTERCRESS
Barbarea vulgaris

Widespread by the sides of
roads and streams. Flowers
May to July.

It is occasionally sold in markets in the USA, where it is cooked as a
green as well as being used as an ingredient of salads. Try picking
the young flowers just before opening in May, and stir-frying them
as broccoli.

WATERCRESS
Rorippa nasturtium-aquaticum

Grows abundantly in and by running water throughout the
British Isles. Flowers from June to October in a bunch of
small white blossoms. Stem hollow and creeping; leaves a
rich, silky green.

Now reduced to a steak-house garnish, watercress was once one of
our most respected green vegetables. It was certainly under small-
scale cultivation by the middle of the eighteenth century, and
quickly became a commercial product as the fast-growing science of
nutrition caught a glimpse of its anti-scorbutic properties (which
result, as we know now, from an exceptionally high Vitamin C content).

Most of the watercress we eat today is grown commercially; but the cultivated plants are identical in every respect to those that grow wild, sometimes in great green hillocks, on the muddy edges of all freshwater streams.

The plants to pick are not the young ones, which are rather tasteless, but the older, sturdier specimens, whose darker leaves have a slight burnish to them. These are the tangy ones, which justify the plant's Latin name, *Nasi-tortium* (meaning 'nose-twisting'). Never pick watercress from stagnant water, or streams which flow through pastureland. It is a host to one stage in the life-cycle of the liver fluke – which can infest humans just as well as sheep. But the larvae are killed by boiling, which is why it is always safest to employ watercress only in cooked dishes.

It will make a good cooked vegetable, especially if spiked with orange and lemon juice and chopped hazelnuts. Simmered with mashed pickled walnuts, it makes a tart sauce for fish.

Watercress soup can be made by boiling two bunches of watercress, roughly chopped, in stock made from two large potatoes, a pint of water and seasoning. Cook for ten minutes, put through a liquidiser, add a little cream if desired, and serve chilled. Finally 'green eggs' can be made by blending the yolks of hard-boiled eggs with a mixture of chopped watercress, grated cheese and mustard, pushing the mixture through a sieve (or blender) and returning it to the yolk cavities.

Watercress

COMMON PENNY CRESS
Thlaspi arvense

> Quite common in arable and waste places. Flowers May to November.

As is the case with all the above wild members of the cabbage family, common penny cress can be used as chickweed, either in salads or as cooked greens.

JACK-BY-THE-HEDGE, GARLIC MUSTARD
Alliaria petiolata

> Widespread and plentiful at the edges of woods and on hedge banks. Small, brilliantly white flowers appear April to June. Leaves: a fresh, bright green, and slightly toothed. Height 1 to 3 feet (30 to 90 cm).

Common Penny Cress   Jack-by-the-hedge

Welcome previews of the spring, the soft leaves of hedge garlic can sometimes be seen as early as February if there has been a mild winter. It is a biennial, and if a warm autumn follows there is often a second crop of new shoots and seedlings in September and October.

For those who like garlic, but only in moderation, Jack-by-the-hedge is ideal as a flavouring. When bruised or chopped the leaves give off just a suspicion of the smell of its unrelated namesake.

Jack-by-the-hedge is a pleasant plant, upright, balanced in colour and classically simple in construction, and only a few leaves should be picked from each specimen. They are useful finely chopped in salads, but best possibly as a sauce for lamb, especially valley lamb which may well have fed on it in low-lying pastures. In the early spring, chop the leaves with hawthorn buds and a little mint, mix well with vinegar and sugar, and serve with the lamb as you would a mint sauce.

There is also a tradition of using garlic mustard with fish. Gerard recommends this; the seventeenth-century herbalist William Giles reports that it was eaten 'as a sauce to salt fish', and in Wales it accompanied herrings.

GOLDEN SAXIFRAGE
Chrysosplenium oppositifolium

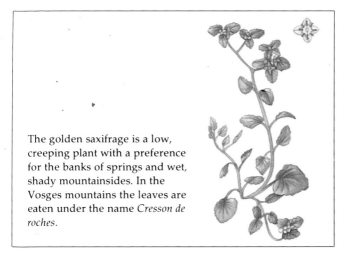

The golden saxifrage is a low, creeping plant with a preference for the banks of springs and wet, shady mountainsides. In the Vosges mountains the leaves are eaten under the name *Cresson de roches*.

It can be used as a green vegetable, but it is not common enough to justify picking, except where plentiful.

MEADOWSWEET
Filipendula ulmaria

Widespread and often abundant throughout the British Isles, by fresh water, in fens and marshy places and damp woods. Flowers June to October, foamy clusters of cream-coloured flowers on stiff, reddish-tinged stems 2 to 4 feet (60 to 120 cm) high. Leaves toothed, dark-green above, silvery grey below.

One of the most summery of all our wild plants. In July the frothy flowerheads of meadowsweet can transform a heavy riverside meadow. The scent of the fresh flowers is warm and heady, that of the crushed leaves more clinically sharp. When dried, both parts of the plant smell of new-mown hay. It was these dried leaves that were used to give an especially aromatic bouquet to port, claret and mead, and it is to this function that the name 'Meadwort' probably refers, not its preference for growing in meadows.

The leaves can be used for flavouring almost any sort of drink and can double for woodruff (p. 120) if that plant is unobtainable. One modern writer recommends it especially as a flavouring for sloe gin.

SALAD BURNET
Poterium sanguisorbum

> Quite common in grassy places on chalk. Flowers May to August.

When crushed the leaves of the salad burnet smell slightly of cucumber. They have long been used as an ingredient of salads, in spite of their diminutive size and slight bitterness, and as a garnish for summer drinks.

A recipe reputedly enjoyed by Napoleon whilst he was in exile on St Helena was a salad of cooked haricot beans, dressed with a generous mixture of olive oil and green herbs – salad burnet (*pimprinelles* in French), tarragon, chives, parsley and chervil.

PARSLEY PIERT
Aphanes arvensis

> Widespread and common on arable and dry ground. Flowers April to October.

Salad Burnet   Parsey Piert

The curious name of this plant probably derives from *perce-pierre*, a plant which breaks through stony ground. So, by sympathetic magic, it came to be used medicinally as a specific against kidney stones. Yet it was Culpeper of all people, herbal wizard extraordinary, who first recommended it as an honest domestic pickle.

Best as a small-scale addition to salads.

WILD ROSE, DOG ROSE
Rosa canina

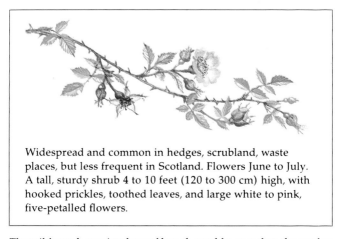

Widespread and common in hedges, scrubland, waste places, but less frequent in Scotland. Flowers June to July. A tall, sturdy shrub 4 to 10 feet (120 to 300 cm) high, with hooked prickles, toothed leaves, and large white to pink, five-petalled flowers.

The wild rose has a simpler and less showy blossom than the garden rose and scarcely droops before it sheds its petals. This is the stage when wild roses should be gathered. Never pick or damage the young flowers. Towards the end of July look for those that have already lost one or two petals, and then gently remove the others into your basket.

Wild roses have a more delicate scent than the garden varieties, but still some of that fleshy, perfumed texture. So if you have only a small quantity, use them neat in salads. Frances Perry once listed ten other uses for the petals: rose wine, rose in brandy, rose vinegar, rhubarb and rose-petal jam, rose honey, rose and coconut candies, Turkish delight, rose drops, crystallised rosepetals, and rose-petal jelly. The list could be extended indefinitely, because the basis of the use of rose-petals, here as elsewhere, is simply as a fragrant improver of well-established dishes. Rose-petal jam is extensively eaten in the Middle East, especially with yoghourt; the recipe below is from Turkey. You will only need to prepare a small potful, as it is exceedingly sweet. And only supplement your wild petals with those from garden roses if it is absolutely necessary to make up the quantity: the thick, fleshy petals of the garden damasks are very difficult to reduce to jelly.

Take two cups of wild rose petals, and make sure that they are free of insects. (Cram them down fairly tightly into the cup when you measure.) Dissolve two cupfuls of sugar in half a cup of water, mixed with one tablespoon each of lemon juice and orange juice. Then stir in the rose petals and put the pan over a very low heat. Stir continuously for about half an hour, or until all the petals have melted. Cool a little, pour into a small glass jar and cover.

ROSE-HIP of WILD ROSE, DOG ROSE
Rosa canina

The fruit is an orange-red, oblong berry, sometimes as much as an inch (2.5 cm) long, and is on the bushes between late August and November.

The fruit of the wild rose, the hip, is the star of one of the great success stories of wild food use. It is the only completely wild fruit which supports a national commercial enterprise – the production of rose-hip syrup.

It was not until the war, when our supplies of citrus fruits were virtually cut off, that the potentialities of rose-hips as a source of Vitamin C were taken seriously. But the fruit had been used as a food for centuries before that. When cultivated fruit was scarce in the Middle Ages, rose-hips were used as a dessert. A recipe from 1730 explains how this hard, unlikely berry was transformed into a filling for tarts. The hips were first slit in half, and the pith and seeds thoroughly cleaned out. Then the skins were put to stand in an earthenware pot until they were soft enough to rub through a sieve. (Notice that this was done without the use of any heat or liquid.)

The resulting purée was mixed with its own weight of sugar, warmed until the sugar melted, and then potted.

But it was not until the Second World War began seriously to disrupt our usual sources of Vitamin C that the government began to consider the use of rose-hips, which had been found to contain twenty times the amount of Vitamin C in oranges. In 1941 the Ministry of Health put forward a scheme for collection, and in that year 120 tons (over 121,000 kg) were gathered by voluntary collectors. The next year the scheme was transferred to the Vegetable Drugs Committee of the Ministry of Supply and 344 tons (349,500 kg) were gathered. By 1943 the redoubtable County Herb Committees were brought in to organise the collection, and for the next three years the harvest averaged 450 tons (over 457,000 kg). The resulting syrup was sold through ordinary retailers at a controlled price of 1s 9d a six-ounce bottle. Mothers and children were able to obtain it in larger quantities, and at reduced prices, from Welfare Clinics.

The syrup is really the beginning of all useful rose-hip recipes, and making it is the simplest way of filtering out the prickly seed, which can be a dangerous internal irritant. Here, as a nostalgic but highly functional guide, are the meticulous directions given by the Ministry of Food during the war for two pounds (900 gm) of hips:

Have ready 3 pints (1.7 litres) of boiling water, mince the hips in a coarse mincer, drop immediately into the boiling water or if possible mince the hips directly into the boiling water and again bring to the boil. Stop heating and place aside for 15 minutes. Pour into a flannel or linen crash jelly bag and allow to drip until the bulk of the liquid has come through. Return the residue to the saucepan, add 1½ pints (852 ml) of boiling water, stir and allow to stand for 10 minutes. Pour back into the jelly bag and allow to drip. To make sure all the sharp hairs are removed put back the first half cupful of liquid and allow to drip through again. Put the mixed juice into a clean saucepan and boil down until the juice measures about 1½ pints (852 ml), then add 1¼ lbs (560 gm) of sugar and boil for a further 5 minutes. Pour into hot sterile bottles and seal at once. If corks are used these should have been boiled for ¼ hour just previously and after insertion coated with melted paraffin wax. It is advisable to use small bottles as the syrup will not keep for more than a week or two once the bottle is opened. Store in a dark cupboard.

Hedgerow Harvest, MoF, 1943

The resulting syrup can be used as a flavouring for milk puddings, ice-cream or almost any sweet, or diluted as a drink.

DEWBERRY
Rubus caesius

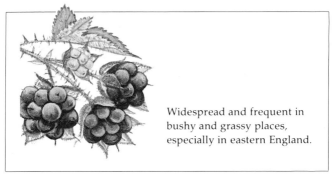

Widespread and frequent in bushy and grassy places, especially in eastern England.

The dewberry carries smaller fruits than the blackberry. They have fewer segments and are covered with a fine bloom. They are also so juicy that they can be difficult to pick without bursting. Take advantage of this juiciness and pick them as a kind of ready-made cocktail cherry. Snip a few of the best berries off with secateurs, together with about 3 inches (7 to 8 cm) of stalk. Serve them with their 'sticks' intact, ready for dipping in bowls of sugar and cream.

BLACKBERRY, BRAMBLE
Rubus fruticosus

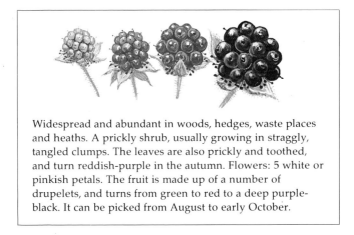

Widespread and abundant in woods, hedges, waste places and heaths. A prickly shrub, usually growing in straggly, tangled clumps. The leaves are also prickly and toothed, and turn reddish-purple in the autumn. Flowers: 5 white or pinkish petals. The fruit is made up of a number of drupelets, and turns from green to red to a deep purple-black. It can be picked from August to early October.

There is little need to write at length about this juicy purple berry, which has been known, loved and picked across the world for generations. Its seeds have even been found in the stomach of a Neolithic man dug up from the Essex clay. Every September, in Europe and America, the commons and scrubland around every big town swarm with pickers, stuffing the berries into mouths and handkerchiefs and polythene bags. Blackberries have a special role in the relationship between townspeople and the countryside. It is not just that they are delicious, and easy to find. Blackberrying carries with it a little of the urban dweller's myth of country life: abundance, harvest, a sense of season, and just enough discomfort to quicken the senses. Maybe it is the scuffing and the scratches that are the real attraction of blackberrying, the proof of satisfying toil against unruly nature.

Everyone has their favourite picking habits and recipes, and these are better guides than anything a book can say. So I will confine myself here to a few of the lesser known facts about the fruit.

Blackberry bushes spread in a curious way. Each cane begins by growing erectly, but then curves downwards until its tip touches the ground. Here the shoot takes root, and a clump of new canes soon forms. The berries themselves grow in large clusters at the end of the older shoots, which die after two or three years' cropping. The lowest berry – right at the tip of the stalk – is the first to ripen, and is the sweetest and fattest of all. Eat it raw. A few weeks later, the other berries near the end ripen; these are less juicy, but are still good for jam and pies. The small berries farther up the stalk often do not ripen until October. They are hard and slightly bitter and are only really useful if cooked with some other fruit.

Even more variety is found from bush to bush. There are reckoned to be at least 400 microspecies in Britain, all differing slightly in flavour, sweetness, fruiting time, nutritional content and size. Blackberries can occur with the savours of grape, plum and even apple. Some varieties have more dietary fibre, weight for weight, than wholemeal bread. If any wild variety does take your fancy, try growing a cutting in the garden. It should bear fruit after a couple of years.

There are any number of recipes which make use of blackberries. They can be made into pies, fruit fools and salads, jellies (they need a little extra pectin), and jams. A good way of serving them fresh is to leave them to steep overnight in red wine.

The most delicious blackberry product I know is a junket made from nothing other than blackberry juice. Remove the juice from the very ripest berries with the help of a juice extractor, or by pressing them through several layers of muslin. Then simply allow the thick, dark juice to stand undisturbed in a warm room. Do not stir or cool the juice, or add anything to it. In a few hours it will have set to the consistency of a light junket, and can be eaten with cream and sweet biscuits.

For cooler days, try an autumn pudding. Make as for summer pudding (see p. 83), but replace the bright red fruits with dark ones – blackberries especially, and also a few stoned sloes and bullaces, elderberries, and chopped crab apples. Cook for about ten minutes and stir in dark honey to taste. Transfer the pulp to a deep pudding basin and pack in slices of brown wholemeal bread until the pulp is covered. Put a weight on top and leave in the refrigerator overnight.

CLOUDBERRY
Rubus chamaemorus

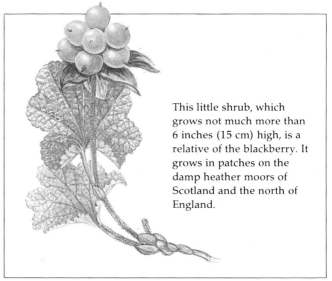

This little shrub, which grows not much more than 6 inches (15 cm) high, is a relative of the blackberry. It grows in patches on the damp heather moors of Scotland and the north of England.

In autumn, the hard berries turn a delicate marmalade orange. They have been used in northern counties for puddings or jams, and could be included in any dish that is conventionally made from blackberries or raspberries.

Sadly, cloudberry has always been a shy fruiter in this country (unlike Scandinavia, for instance). In the Berwyn mountains in Wales, an unusual tradition commemorated this scarcity, and persisted up till the end of the last century. Shepherds from Llanrhaiadr believed that a quart of cloudberries was the wage which St Dogfan was due for his spiritual ministry, and anyone who could bring such a quantity to the parson on St Dogfan's days had his tithes remitted for the year.

RASPBERRY
Rubus idaeus

Widespread throughout the British Isles, and quite frequent in hedgerows, rocky woods, and heaths. A slender shrub, with usually unbranched arching stems growing up to 6 feet (1.8 m) high, and only very slightly spiny. Leaves toothed and oval, and often whitish below. Flowers small and white in drooping clusters. Fruit from July to September, a rich red berry, formed by a number of drupelets.

The raspberry is usually the first soft fruit to ripen, occasionally as early as the last weeks of June. If you have difficulty distinguishing young raspberries from unripe blackberries, look at the stems on which they are growing. The raspberry has woody, cane-like stems, comparatively smooth except for a few weak prickles; the blackberry has much coarser stems armed with a great number of strong prickles.

Although many raspberry plants growing in the wild are bird-seeded from cultivated stock, the fruit is as authentic a British native as its close relative the blackberry (see p. 79). It is not difficult to see why, of the two, it was the raspberry that was taken into gardens. It grows more tidily and with greater restraint than the spiny, aggressive bramble. And this of course means that it has been less prolific in the wild – another good reason for nurturing the plant in the non-competitive security of the garden.

Raspberries are such a rich and substantial fruit that it would be a waste to make jelly from them. But simmered in their own juice for about a quarter of an hour, and then boiled to setting point with an equal weight of sugar, they make a very fine jam.

If you only find a handful of wild berries, use them for stuffing game birds, or to make the famous summer pudding. This needs no cooking, but must be made the day before it is needed. Cut some fairly thick slices of bread and remove the crusts. Moisten them with milk, and line the sides and bottom of a deep pudding basin with them. (Make sure that the slices overlap well, so that they will hold together when turned out.) Then fill the pudding basin with a mixture of cooked raspberries and any red, white or black currants that are available. Cover the top with more slices of moistened bread, and then with greaseproof paper. Put a weight on top of the paper and leave the pudding to stand in the refrigerator overnight.

Raspberry vinegar, made by soaking ½ lb (225 gm) of fruit in a pint (568 ml) of white wine vinegar for three days, is an important ingredient of *nouvelle cuisine*. But long before that it was a popular domestic remedy for 'tickly' throats.

WILD STRAWBERRY
Fragaria vesca

Widespread and common on grassy banks, heaths, open woods. A low, creeping plant with hairy runners and stalks. The leaves are in groups of three, toothed, shiny green above, and silky grey beneath. Fruits, late June to August, small drooping red berries with the seeds protruding.

In some parts of the country wild strawberries are abundant, and carpet wide patches of dry and heathy ground. But normally you will need to search carefully for them, looking for the trefoil leaves in the bracken edges and rough grass. The drooping berries can be even more elusive and are often completely hidden by the leaves.

The best wild strawberries are those eaten straight from plants growing on bare limestone. The fruits will have been warmed up by

Wild Strawberry

the sun reflected from the rock, and their fragrance can be savoured to the full.

The most useful recipes are those which make the best of small quantities of berries. Try a bowlful topped with champagne. Add a few to a fresh fruit salad. Or make use of their winy aroma by turning them into a sauce for other fruit, or for green salads. Simply purée them with a little wine and seasoning.

SILVERWEED
Potentilla anserina

> An abundant flower of damp grassy and waste places. The undersides of the leaves are flashed with a pale matt grey, making the plant look withered before its time. Upper surface silky, liquid green.

The roots were cultivated as a crop from late prehistoric times. In upland areas of Britain they were eaten right up until the introduction of the potato – and later, in times of famine, though they are a meagre and not very flavoursome root.

The leaves were once used by foot soldiers as an apparently cooling lining for their boots.

Silverweed

Herb Bennet

HERB BENNET
Geum urbanum

An undistinguished plant, yet it is pleasant in late summer to find its small 5-petalled yellow flowers on an otherwise dark woodland floor.

The clove-like odour of the roots of herb bennet, or wood avens, was once reputed to repel moths; yet it clearly attracted human beings, for it was widely grown as a pot-herb in the sixteenth century. As well as its many medicinal uses (against 'the stings of venomous beasts') it was also added to broths and soups.

BITTER VETCH
Lathyrus montanus

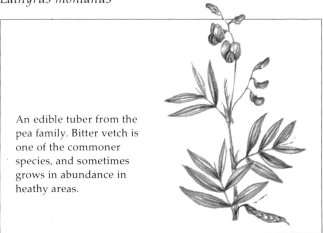

An edible tuber from the
pea family. Bitter vetch is
one of the commoner
species, and sometimes
grows in abundance in
heathy areas.

It has been recognised as a vegetable since at least the Middle Ages.
In later times the roots have been used as a subsistence crop in the
Scottish islands, either raw or dried. They have also been used for
flavouring whisky.

REST-HARROW
Ononis repens

A common enough plant in dry and
chalky grassland, but too handsome
to pick needlessly. It is like a sweet
pea bred for the rockery: short, pert
and bushy.

In the north children would dig it up and chew it; hence it acquired
the names wild liquorice and spanish root.

WOOD-SORREL
Oxalis acetosella

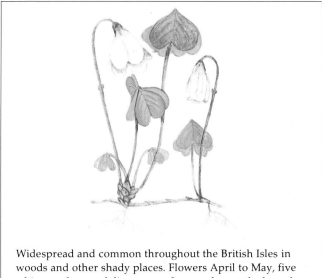

Widespread and common throughout the British Isles in woods and other shady places. Flowers April to May, five white petals on a delicate stem. Leaves shamrock-shaped, and lime green when young. 2 to 4 inches (5 to 10 cm) high.

On the dark, barren floors of conifer woods, the leaves of the wood-sorrel – often the only plant growing there in the spring – lie in scattered clusters amongst the needles, like fretwork. They are folded to begin with, in the shape of some episcopal hat, then open flat, three hearts with their points joined at the stem.

Wood-sorrel was being used as a salad vegetable certainly as early as the fourteenth century. By the fifteenth it was under cultivation, and John Evelyn recommended it in a list of plants suitable for kitchen gardens.

Its use then was as an ingredient for salads, or pulped as a sharpening ingredient for sauces. It can be used the same way today, but sparingly, since it contains certain oxalates which are not too good for the body in large quantities. It is these salts which are responsible for the plant's pleasantly sharp taste, which is not unlike the skins of grapes.

The American Indians apparently fed the roots of this plant to their horses to increase their speed.

SPURGE
Euphorbia species

POISONOUS

Sun Spurge

Modest-looking plants, commonly regarded as weeds. Yellowish-green flowers from April to September, depending on the species.

Petty Spurge

Dwarf Spurge

The majority of our native spurges are poisonous. They exude a milky juice which can produce intense irritation of the lips and mouth, and act as a drastic purgative if swallowed. **Sun spurge**, *Euphorbia helioscopia*, **dwarf spurge**, *Euphorbia exigua*, and **petty spurge**, *Euphorbia peplus*, are the commonest species.

DOG'S MERCURY
Mercurialis perennis

POISONOUS

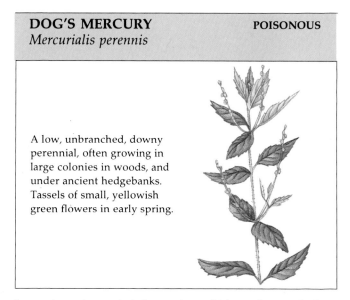

A low, unbranched, downy perennial, often growing in large colonies in woods, and under ancient hedgebanks. Tassels of small, yellowish green flowers in early spring.

It contains an intensely irritant poison which can damage the liver and kidneys as well as the stomach.

JEWEL-WEED
Impatiens capensis

The jewel-weed or orange balsam is an increasingly frequent plant along the banks of rivers and canals in the south of England. It can often form magnificent bushes, up to 4 feet (120 cm) high and festooned with mottled orange, nasturtium-like bells.

Jewel-weed is an introduction from North America and was not found in the wild in this country until 1822. In its native land the young leaves and stems were used as a vegetable.

The green seed pods and seeds of another immigrant balsam, the Himalayan balsam, *Impatiens glandulifera*, are also eaten in their native Asian habitats. They make a refreshingly nutty snack.

RED CURRANT
Ribes rubrum

Widespread but local in woods and hedgerows, especially
by streams and fens. A bush, 2 to 4 feet (60 to 120 cm)
high, with toothed leaves broken into 3 or 5 lobes. Flowers:
small, green and drooping. Fruits from July, round and
shiny red, with a slightly translucent skin.

Some red currant bushes are blatant escapes from nearby gardens.
But the plant is an authentic native, and truly wild specimens are not
uncommon in old woodland, by stream banks and in rough fens.
(Avoid confusion with the cloying fruit of guelder rose. This is also a
shrub of woods and riversides, but its berries lack a 'tail' and look
heavy and waxy beside the almost translucent skins of the red currant.)

Red currrants make a good jelly, provided the rather obtrusive
pips are strained out. But given that you will probably only find a
few, they may be best eaten as a bracing field-snack, in what the fruit
gourmet Edward Bunyard described as 'ambulant consumption'.

BLACK CURRANT
Ribes nigrum

Grows wild in damp woodland across the whole of Europe.
Stems and leaves issue heavy and characteristic smell.
Dangling clusters of berries appear in June, ripening in
July.

The soothing properties of black currant juice were probably
known long before the plant passed into cultivation, for it was often
given against sore throats and 'the quinsy'. It is a rather uncommon
plant in the wild, and can readily be told from red currant by its
larger, heavily aromatic leaves. A few of these, dried, can transform
a pot of Indian tea.

The currants can also be dried, and in this form they are one of the
bases of pemmican, an Amerindian dish taken up by polar explorers. The currants are pounded together with dried meat, and the
mixture bound together and coated with fat or tallow. The result
was a food containing almost all the ingredients necessary for a balanced diet, which would keep well even on long journeys.

GOOSEBERRY
Ribes uva-crispa

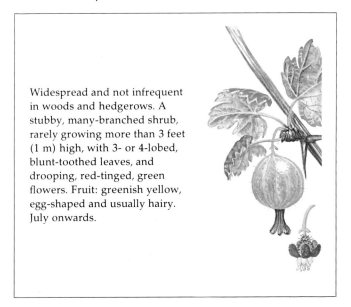

Widespread and not infrequent in woods and hedgerows. A stubby, many-branched shrub, rarely growing more than 3 feet (1 m) high, with 3- or 4-lobed, blunt-toothed leaves, and drooping, red-tinged, green flowers. Fruit: greenish yellow, egg-shaped and usually hairy. July onwards.

In some areas of the north, the hedges can be thick with goose-berries, and with the help of a pair of gloves you should be able to pick a fair quantity.

Depending on their ripeness and sweetness they can be used in any of the recipes which normally employ the cultivated fruit. The ripe berries make gooseberry pie or gooseberry fool, the underripe ones gooseberry jelly. (See the recipe with elder flowers on p. 44.)

Oldbury tarts, from Oldbury-on-Severn, were traditionally made with wild gooseberries and sold at the Whitsuntide fairs (though the berries can hardly have been ripe at this time, and preserved fruit must have been used). The tarts were actually small pies, tea-cup sized, filled with gooseberries and demerara sugar.

A more practical recipe, and one which can be followed with a small quantity of berries, is for a fennel and gooseberry sauce for mackerel. Stew a handful of fruit in a little cider, pulp through a sieve, then mix with chopped fennel (p. 112) and mustard and honey to taste.

COMMON MALLOW
Malva sylvestris

Widespread and abundant on banks, roadsides and waste places, especially near the sea. Rather less common in Scotland. Flowers from June to October, five-petalled, purplish blossoms up to 1 inch (2.5 cm) across. The plant is coarse, bushy and often straggly, and carries crinkly, ivy-shaped leaves which are slightly clammy to touch when young.

Mallow blooms late into the autumn, and its flowers have a strange, artificial elegance that is unexpected in such an obviously hardy wayside weed. The mauve petals are arched like some porcelain decoration, and veined with deep purple streaks.

The leaves stay green and fresh almost all the year, but are best picked in the summer months, when they can be stretched like films of gelatine. Always wash the leaves well and discard any that have developed a brownish rust, or are embedded with tiny black insect eggs.

Mallow leaves can be cooked as a spinach, but they are extremely glutinous, and a more attractive way of using them is to make them into soup. In Arab countries the leaves of a similar species are the basis of the famous soup, melokhia:

Melokhia is one of Egypt's national dishes. It is an ancient peasant soup, the making of which is believed to be portrayed in pharaonic tomb paintings. The medieval melokhia seems to have been a little richer, incorporating fried minced meat and chicken. Today, only a few families add these. . . . Peasant women prepare this soup almost daily. Protein stock is too expensive, so they cook the leaves in water in which a few vegetables have been boiled. The leaves give the soup a glutinous texture. The women cook the soup in large pots, which they carry to the fields on their heads for the men to eat at midday. When the work is done and the men come home, they eat it again at dusk with equal pleasure. Melokhia has recently acquired a symbolic and patriotic importance in Egypt, for it represents the national, popular taste as opposed to the more snobbish and cosmopolitan taste of the old regime. Most families have their own special way of preparing it, and the proportions vary according to the financial means, position and preferences of the people who make it.

from *Middle Eastern Food*, by Claudia Roden

To make a fairly authentic version of melokhia in this country, take about a pound (450 gms) of young mallow leaves, cut off the stalks, wash well, and chop very small or purée in a blender. Boil in about two pints (just over a litre) of chicken stock for ten minutes. Then prepare a garlic sauce by frying two crushed cloves of garlic in a little oil until golden brown, adding a dessertspoonful of ground coriander, a pinch of cayenne pepper, and some salt, and mixing to a paste in the hot pan. Add this paste to the soup, cover the saucepan tightly and simmer for two or three minutes, stirring occasionally to prevent the leaves falling to the bottom.

The melokhia can then be served on its own, or with boiled rice, or pieces of cooked meat and vegetables.

Common mallow is also known for its small, round seeds, called 'cheeses' (from their taste, which is mildly nutty). Children in country districts still pick and eat these, though they're such a diminutive mouthful that their taste and texture are hardly noticeable. Some experimenters have found that modern children are more attracted by the leaves, deep-fried in hot oil until they resemble a wafer-thin green crisp!

MARSH MALLOW
Althaea officinalis

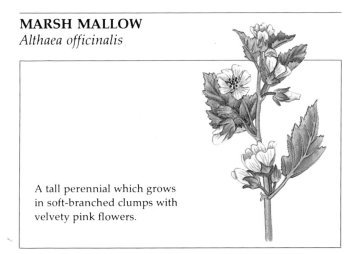

A tall perennial which grows in soft-branched clumps with velvety pink flowers.

The plant that gave the sweet its name. Today marshmallow is made from starch, gelatine and sugar. But it was once produced from the roots of *Althaea officinalis*, which contain not only their own starch, but also albumen, a crystallisable sugar, a fixed oil and a good deal of gelatinous matter. They were gathered by fishermen's wives in the dykes and saltmarshes of the east coast.

SWEET VIOLET
Viola odorata

The sweet violet is fairly common in hedgebanks and shady places, though less frequent than the odourless dog violet. Pinkish, sweet-smelling flowers from March to May.

In the past its flowers were used quite extensively in cooking for their fragrance and decorative qualities. They were one of the ingredients of the Salmagundy. In the fourteenth century they were beaten up with a ground rice pudding flavoured with ground almonds and cream. Much later, after émigrés from the French Revolution had made veal popular in this country, they were used as one of the elaborate floral dressings for joints of that meat. They are best known, though, as the crystallised sweets.

LARGE EVENING PRIMROSE
Oenothera erythrosepala

A tall, downy flower with a fine poppy-like yellow blossom.

Large Evening Primrose

It was introduced from America into Britain in the early seventeenth century, and was soon taken into gardens for its roots, which were eaten boiled. In Germany the young shoots were also eaten.

ROSE BAY
Epilobium angustifolium

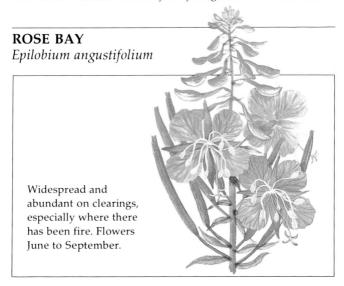

Widespread and abundant on clearings, especially where there has been fire. Flowers June to September.

The young shoots have been eaten like asparagus in parts of America and Northern Europe, though they are very bitter.

DWARF CORNEL
Chamaepericlymenum suecicum

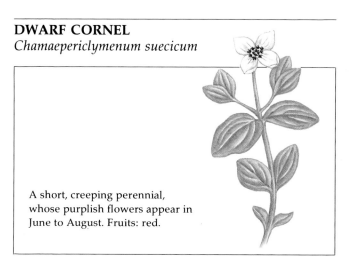

A short, creeping perennial, whose purplish flowers appear in June to August. Fruits: red.

The one aperitif in this book. The small scarlet berries used to be munched by the Highlanders to stimulate their appetites. In America they have been eaten by the Indians, and occasionally made into puddings.

Dwarf cornel is rare, and there are more agreeable ways to perk up your appetite, so this tiny plant is better left unpicked. Only in a few areas in the Highlands does it still thrive under the shelter of heather and bilberry.

COW PARSLEY
Anthriscus sylvestris

Widespread and abundant on footpaths, roadsides, banks etc. Flowers April to June, umbels of tiny white flowers. The plant is 2 to 4 feet (60 to 120 cm) high, with hollow, green, furrowed stems, hairy near the bottom of the plant but smooth above. The leaves are grass-green, slightly downy, and much divided, looking very like wedge-shaped ferns.

No plant shapes our roadside landscape more than cow parsley. In May its lacy white flowers teem along every path and hedgebank. It grows prolifically; road verges can be blanketed with it for miles on end, and be broadened several feet by its overhanging foliage.

Yet it has been almost totally overlooked as a herb, even though one of its less common botanical names is wild chervil. It is in fact the closest wild relative of cultivated chervil, *Anthriscus cerefolium*, a little coarser than that garden variety, maybe, but sharing the same fresh, spicy flavour.

Cow parsley is the first common umbellifer to come into flower in the spring, and this is often enough to identify it positively. But since there are a number of related species which resemble it, and which can cause serious poisoning, I have included below some notes on the characteristics which unequivocally identify cow parsley. The most dangerous sources of confusion are fool's parsley and hemlock.

Cow parsley grows up to 4 feet (120 cm) tall, and never as high as hemlock's 7 or more feet (over 210 cm). Fool's parsley is an altogether more flimsy shrub, rarely exceeding 1 foot (30 cm). Its stem is stout, furrowed and slightly hairy, as against hemlock's purple spotted stems. And it lacks both hemlock's offensive mousy smell, and fool's parsley's drooping green bracts beneath the flower heads.

You should pick cow parsley as soon as the stems are sufficiently developed for you to identify it. Later in the year it becomes rather bitter. It dries well, so pick enough to last you through the off-

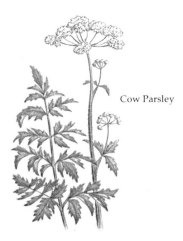

Cow Parsley

season as well as for your immediate needs. But do not gather the plant from the sides of major roads; even if it has been spared the Highway Department's herbicides, it will certainly have been contaminated by car exhausts.

Chervil is a very versatile herb and small quantities make a lively addition to most sorts of salads, particularly cold potato, tomato, and cucumber. It also makes a good flavouring for hot haricot beans and herb omelettes.

Cow parsley is a biennial and next year's leaves appear in the autumn and remain green throughout the winter, and those experienced enough to tell the plant from its leaves alone could do worse than pick some fresh for winter soups and casseroles. It goes well with hot baked potatoes, and as an addition to the French country dish cassoulet.

CORIANDER
Coriandrum sativum

When you come across a green coriander plant, it is difficult to believe that it will eventually produce those warmly aromatic seeds that are used so extensively in curries. It is a hairless annual which grows up to 50 cm tall, bearing white flowers which appear in May to June.

The flavour of the green leaves is strong, slightly soapy and reminiscent of rue (*Coriandrum* derives from the Greek word for 'bug'). But the smell and taste can grow on you, and the green leaves are popular additions to salads in the Middle East.

Coriander grows wild in a few scattered places in the British Isles (even alongside the M1), and was probably brought here from its native Mediterranean habitat by the Romans. The dried seeds are mentioned in Exodus and are one of the oldest spices known to man. Ground up, they are an essential ingredient of most curries, and will add a subtle flavour to soups, and, above all, to pork dishes. Len Deighton's recommendation: 'Hurl crushed coriander seeds into any open pot you see.'

PIGNUT
Conopodium majus

> This plant, a slender, feathery umbellifer, is still common in June, and July in woods, meadows and sandy heaths, but of course should not be dug up except on your own land.

The custom of grubbing for pig or earth nuts seems to have died out now, even amongst children. There was a time when they were one of the most popular of wayside nibbles, even though extracting them from the ground was as delicate a business as an egg and spoon race. They cannot be pulled out, for the thin leaf stalk breaks off very quickly. The fine white roots must be unearthed with a knife, and carefully traced down to the tuber.

The 'nuts' can be eaten raw, once they have been scraped or washed, though one early botanist recommended them peeled and boiled in broth with pepper.

PARSLEY
Petroselinum crispum

> A sturdy plant, similar to the familiar garden herb, but lacking its thick, feathery leaf clusters.

It is doubtful whether any of the parsley plants which can occasionally be found growing wild on rocky places near the sea are any more than escapees from gardens. The plant is almost certainly a comparatively recent introduction from the Mediterranean, and I can find no records of it being grown here before the sixteenth century.

As a change from a redundant garnishing, try frying parsley for half a minute in hot butter, and serving it as a vegetable with fish. It is extremely rich in Vitamin C.

Pignut

Parsley

SWEET CICELY
Myrrhis odorata

Quite common on waysides and
stream banks in the north of
England and Scotland. Flowers
May to July, large umbels of
white flowers. Grows to 4 or 5
feet (120 to 150 cm) tall, with
elegant, feathery, aniseed-
scented foliage.

Cicely is one of the few plants where the connotation 'sweet' refers
as much to taste as to scent. The leaves have distinctly sugary overtones to their mild aniseed flavour, and are ideal for flavouring
stewed fruits such as gooseberries and plums. In France, the young
leaf sprays are dipped in batter and fried as an *hors d'oeuvres*.

A simpler and more accessible starter are the long green seeds
eaten straight from the plant in June. They are up to an inch (2.5 cm)
long and resemble miniature gherkins. Their crisp texture and
sweet-and-sour flavour make them an excellent wayside nibble.
Gerard thought the seeds the plant's choicest part: 'eaten as a sallad
whilest they are yet greene, with oyle, vinegar and pepper, they
exceed all other sallads by many degrees, both in pleasantness of
taste, sweetnesse of smell, and wholesomeness for the cold and
feeble stomack'.

SEA HOLLY
Eryngium maritimum

A thistle-like plant, its spiny, ice-blue leaves covered with
bloom and ribbed and edged with a fine white tracery of
veins. It likes the rough ground of sandy and shingly
beaches, and its roots have consequently been confused

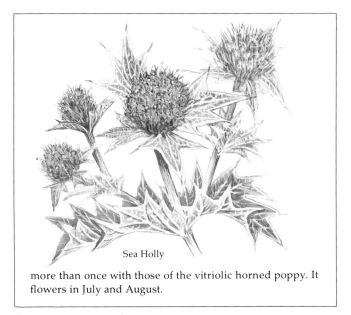

Sea Holly

more than once with those of the vitriolic horned poppy. It flowers in July and August.

Sea holly roots, as Eryngo roots, were once extensively used for making candied sweetmeats. The roots were dug up (they could be up to 6 feet (1.8 m) long) in the spring or autumn, partly boiled until they could be peeled and then cut into thin slices. These were cooked with an equal weight of sugar until the latter became syrup, when the roots were removed and allowed to cool.

Candied Eryngo roots were a vital ingredient of that redoubtable Elizabethan dish, marrow-bone pie. They were also roasted, when they acquired something of the flavour of chestnuts.

GROUND ELDER
Aegopodium podagraria

Widespread and common in shady places under hedges, in gardens, etc. Occurs throughout the British Isles. Flowers June to August, white umbels on a creeping, hairless stem, never much more than 1 to 2 feet (30 to 60 cm) high. Leaves: finely toothed, in groups of three at the end of the leaf stems.

Ground Elder

Neither an ash nor an elder, goutweed's leaves do bear a superficial resemblance to both these trees. It can often be found in quite large patches by roadsides and under garden hedges, its pale green leaves making a bright carpet in the shady places. Its continued presence in both habitats is a telling example of the persistence of some weeds in places where they were once cultivated and valued.

Ground elder was probably introduced to this country by the Romans. In the Middle Ages it was grown in gardens as a vegetable, and at roadside inns and monasteries as a quick palliative for travellers' gout. Advances in medical understanding put paid to the second of these functions and the growing preference for bland-tasting vegetables to the first. Any popularity it still retained was finally undermined by the imperialistic tendencies of its rootstock, which would quickly take over its host's garden. Even in the sixteenth century, when the plant was still being used as a pot-herb, John Gerard wrote complainingly of it: 'once taken roote, it will hardly be gotten out again, spoiling and getting every yeere more ground, to the annoying of better herbes.'

Still, it is an agreeable vegetable cooked like spinach, with an unusual tangy flavour.

FOOL'S PARSLEY
Aethusa cynapium   **POISONOUS**

A low, weak, hairless annual, often growing as a weed in gardens and other cultivated ground. Parsley-like foliage, and flowers in white umbels, over a distinctive ring of bracts which makes them look bearded.

The plant has a distasteful smell which puts off most pickers, but poisoning has occasionally occurred. It is rarely fatal in healthy subjects.

HOGWEED, COW PARSNIP
Heracleum sphondylium

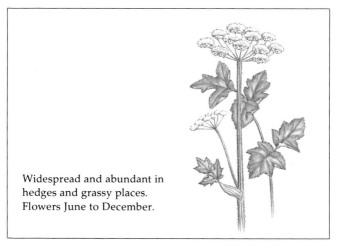

Widespread and abundant in hedges and grassy places. Flowers June to December.

Cooked like asparagus the young shoots are marvellously fleshy.

HEMLOCK   POISONOUS
Conium maculataum

Common on waste ground and by streams. Flowers June,
July, in white umbels. A tall plant, up to 5 feet (150 cm)
high, with feathery foliage and hollow, purple-spotted
stems. The whole plant emits an unpleasant mousy odour
when bruised. Most toxic when young and green, and the
poisonous alkaloids are destroyed by drying and heat.

THE WATER DROPWORTS   POISONOUS
Oenanthe species

Responsible for the majority of fatalities from wild plant
poisoning in this country – often from European visitors
mistaking the roots for parsnips, etc. ALL species –
including **Tubular water dropwort**, *O. Fistulosa*, **Fine-leaved
water dropwort**, *O. aquatica*, and **Parsley water-dropwort**,
O. lachenalii – are deadly poisonous, often rapidly and
suddenly.

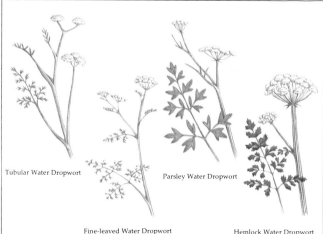

Tubular Water Dropwort

Parsley Water Dropwort

Fine-leaved Water Dropwort

Hemlock Water Dropwort

The commonest and most widespread species is **Hemlock water dropwort**, *Oenanthe crocata*. Widespread and locally common in or by fresh water. Flowers June to August, large white umbels. A stout, hairless plant, up to 4 feet (120 cm) high, often forming clumps. Stem is usually hollow, and the foliage glossy, divided and smelling pleasantly of parsley.

WILD CELERY
Apium graveolens

Widespread but local in damp places near the sea, and mainly in the south and east of England. Flowers June to September. A strongly-smelling plant, growing about 1 to 2 feet (30 to 60 cm) high, with shiny, yellow-green leaves, shaped much like those of garden celery, and rather sparse white umbels of flowers.

The powerful aroma of wild celery, or smallage, largely disappears on drying, leaving a herb which is exactly like strong celery in flavour, and ideal for soups. To make a straight cream of wild celery much richer and tangier than garden celery soup, pick a small bunch of the leaves, dry for about three weeks (in a little-used room!), then simmer for about half an hour in some chicken stock. Strain, stir in a cupful of hot milk and serve immediately.

But even in the fresh, undried state, the taste is nothing like as powerful as might be expected. The stems are not of course as bity as those of the garden variety, but I have found that a few of them, chopped, make a brisk ingredient for salads.

LOVAGE
Ligusticum scoticum

A stocky umbelliferate with bright green, leathery leaves, which grows locally on rocky sea cliffs in Scotland. It was occasionally eaten against scurvy.

Its cultivated cousin, *Ligusticum officinale*, is naturalised from herb gardens in a few places. This domesticated lovage is a much more distinctive plant, growing 11 or 12 feet (over 3.5 m) tall, and its uses are correspondingly wider. The hollow stems have been candied like angelica, and blanched like celery for use as a salad vegetable.

The flavour of both varieties is curious, basically resembling celery, but having quite strong yeasty overtones. Because of this lovage has been used to add body to the flavour of soups and casseroles when meat is short.

Lovage is scarce in the wild, and the best way of experiencing its flavour may be to grow *Ligusticum officinale* in the herb garden – though it is a very large perennial.

WILD PARSNIP
Pastinaca sativa

The wild parsnip is a stocky, economical plant, with none of the excess and luxuriance of some of our umbelliferae. In the poor soils of road verges and waste ground it often grows to no more than 18 inches (45 cm) in height. Its chrome yellow umbels could only really be confused with those of fennel (see p. 109) which is instantly distinguishable by its feathery leaves and aniseed smell, as well as being strongly flavoured, also rather thin and wiry, in spite of being a biennial and having two years to grow from seed to flowering maturity.

Pastinaca sativa is almost certainly an ancestor of our cultivated parsnips. An experiment in Cirencester in the mid-nineteenth century produced large, fleshy roots from the wild stock in ten years. No more was done than to transplant the wild parsnips into rich garden soil, and resow each season with the seeds of those specimens with the largest roots.

Cultivation of this kind was almost certainly under way in the Middle Ages, as the parsnip was valued as a sweetening ingredient for sauces, cakes and puddings.

The wild roots are just about edible after the first frosts but they are thin and wiry and of more historical than culinary interest.

ALEXANDERS
Smyrnium olustratum

Widespread and locally abundant in hedgebanks and waste places, especially near the sea. Flowers April to June, umbels of yellow-green flowers. A bushy, solid-stemmed hairless plant growing up to 4 feet (120 cm) high. Leaves glossy, toothed, on groups of three at the end of the leaf stalk; the other end being joined to the main stem by a substantial sheath.

The Romans brought alexanders to this country from the Mediterranean, as a pot-herb. It thrived, became naturalised, and was still being planted in kitchen gardens in the early eighteenth century.

Today it is widely naturalised in hedgebanks near the coast. It sprouts early and rapidly in the spring, and its bright, glossy leaves can sometimes be seen pushing through the January snows.

The most succulent part of the plant is the stem. You should cut those leaf stems which grow near the base of the plant, where they are thick and have been partially blanched by the surrounding grass or the plant's own foliage. You should be able to cut about six inches (15 cm) of pinkish stalk from each stem (discarding the greener bits). Don't be put off by the plant's rather cloying angelica smell; this disappears almost completely with cooking.

Cook these stems in boiling water for not more than ten minutes. Then eat them like asparagus, with molten butter. They have a delicate texture, and a pleasantly aromatic taste. The young leaves make a spicy addition to salads, and the flower-buds can be pickled.

ROCK SAMPHIRE
Crithmum maritimum

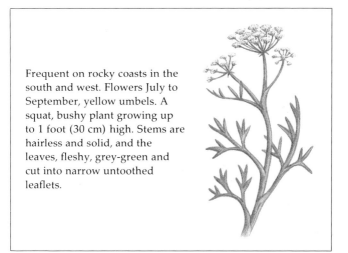

Frequent on rocky coasts in the south and west. Flowers July to September, yellow umbels. A squat, bushy plant growing up to 1 foot (30 cm) high. Stems are hairless and solid, and the leaves, fleshy, grey-green and cut into narrow untoothed leaflets.

The plant grows quite frequently in shingle, and you can often find it by its smell alone, warm but slightly sulphurous. Both stems and leaves can be used, but before cooking remove any leaves that have begun to turn slimy, and any hard parts of the stalk. Then boil in water for about ten minutes, and serve with melted butter. To eat, suck the fleshy parts away from the stringy veins.

The most curious recipe I have come across for this vegetable dates from the mid-seventeenth century, and is for a samphire hash. Take about a quarter of a pound (112 gm) of chopped samphire and mix with a handful of diced pickled cucumbers and some capers. Boil in a pint of stock to which has been added two tablespoons of wine vinegar, the juice and grated peel of one lemon, pepper and nutmeg. Simmer for half an hour. Take off the boil and gradually add slivers of butter and the yolk of an egg, stirring continuously, until the mixture thickens.

This sauce was used as a garnish for meat, and the whole dish dressed with fresh samphire leaves and bright red barberries.

FENNEL
Foeniculum vulgare

Locally distributed throughout
the south of England,
Midlands, East Anglia and
Wales. Less common in the
north and Scotland. Occurs on
cliffs, waste ground and damp
places,especially near the sea.
Flowers early June to October;
clusters of mustard yellow
blossoms; leaves threadlike
and aromatic. Height up to 5
feet (1.5 m).

See fennel's feathery sprays along damp coastal roadsides in early
July, and you will understand the attraction it held for the early
herbalists. Its umbels of yellow flowers and smooth, threadlike
leaves are elegantly soft, giving the plant a curiously foppish air
beside the hairy yokels it shares living space with. Crush the leaves
in your hand and they give off a powerful aromatic odour, reminiscent of aniseed. On a hot summer's day this is enough to betray the
plant's presence, for the cool tang stands out from the heavy, sweet
musk of hogweed and elder like a throwback to a sharp April
morning.

Fennel occurs throughout the southern half of the British Isles, on
cliffs as much as in dank meadows, but it tends to grow in rather
localised patches. All parts of the plant are edible, from the stalks – if
your teeth are strong enough – to the rather sparse bulb. (The larger
fennel bulbs obtainable from some greengrocers belong to cultivated Florence fennel, *Foeniculum vulgare* var. *dulce*.) They all have a
fresh, nutty flavour. But it is the thinner stalks, leaf sprays and seeds
that are the most useful.

The green parts of the plant should be cut with a sharp knife as
early in the summer as possible, and some (stalks included) hung
up to dry for the winter. Fennel smells stronger as it dries, and after
a few weeks a good-sized bunch will be powerful enough to scent a

whole room. The seeds should be gathered late in October, just before they are fully dry.

Although fennel seeds are still mentioned in the British Pharmaceutical Codex as a remedy for 'winde' (no doubt the reason they are chewed after Indian meals), a more reliable range of uses today is as flavouring for fish dishes. Fennel is especially good with oily fish, though the tradition of using it in this way probably derives from nothing more than the plant's preference for coastal areas. The dried stalks form the basis of the famous Provençal red mullet dish, *rouget flambé au fenouil*. The finely chopped green leaves are also good to add to liver, potato salad, parsnips, and even, Len Deighton recommends, apple pie.

A dish that can really charm and make use of the cool fragrance of fennel is okrochka, an exotic cold soup from Greece. It is a perfect dish on a warm evening, and utilises some other wild summer herbs you may gather.

Mix two cartons of yoghourt (plain or apple) with roughly the same quantity of milk in a sizeable bowl. Add one cup of diced fresh cucumber, ½ cup of chopped pickled cucumber or gherkin, ½ cup of diced cooked chicken, and a handful of finely chopped fennel leaves. Add any other summer herbs that you have available – mint, parsley and chives are particularly good – but they must be fresh, and not in such quantities that they mask the fennel. Season with salt and freshly ground pepper and put in the fridge for at least two hours.

Before serving, add two roughly chopped hard-boiled eggs to the soup, and sprinkle the surface with a little more black pepper and fresh herbs.

HEATHER
Calluna vulgaris

Widespread and abundant on heaths, moors, and in dry, open woods. Flowers August to September. A stubby, evergreen shrub 6 to 18 inches (15 to 45 cm) high, with numerous tiny leaves in opposite rows. The flowers are purple and bell-shaped and carried in spikes.

Heather is a tenacious and aggressive plant and completely carpets huge areas of moorland. Trample on it and you will make no impression on its wiry stems. Even extensive burning only sets it

Heather

back temporarily, and within a couple of years new shoots spring up beside the blackened branches of the old.

Heather has an abundant range of economic uses. It provides food for sheep and grouse, material for fuel, thatching, basketwork and brooms, and an orange dye. In some places it was used for flavouring ale, and in a modern recipe from the Orkneys, it replaces hops in a conventional beer recipe in the proportions of: 1 gallon (4.5 litres) heather tops to 2 lbs (900 gm) malt extract, 1½ lbs (675 gm) sugar and 2 gallons (9.10 litres) water.

The dried flower heads make a good tea, and Robert Burns is supposed to have drunk a 'Moorland Tea' based on heather tops mixed with the dried leaves of bilberry, blackberry, speedwell, thyme and wild strawberry.

BILBERRY
Vaccinium myrtillus

Widespread throughout the British Isles, except the south and east of England, and locally abundant on heaths and moors. An erect shrub, growing 9 to 18 inches (22 to 44 cm) high, with hairless twigs and oval, slightly toothed, bright green leaves. Flowers: solitary, drooping, greenish-pink globes. Fruits from July to September, small, round and black, and covered with bloom.

The bilberry is an intriguingly juicy and versatile fruit, and would doubtless be more popular commercially if picking it were not such a laborious business. The shrub grows low, often largely concealed by dense heather, and the berries form in nothing like the concentrations of, say, blackberries. So even on the moors where the bush grows in abundance, gathering any quantity can involve the thorough searching of a fair-sized patch of land. On parts of the Continent, bilberry gathering has been partially mechanised with the help of a large combing device known as a *peigne*, though this takes away much of the fun of hunting for the berries – the discovery of clusters under the leaves, the bloom rubbing away on one's fingers.

Some of the most interesting bilberry recipes come from Yorkshire, where the pies are known as 'mucky-mouth pies' and are a feature of funeral teas. One classic local recipe sets the berries in a kind of Yorkshire pudding. Make batter in the usual way, but add 2 tablespoons of brown sugar for every 4 ozs (115 gm) of flour, and then stir in 8 ozs (230 gm) bilberries. Bake in a medium oven for half an hour.

Another Yorkshire touch with bilberries is to add a few sprigs of mint to the stewed fruit and jams. The two flavours complement each other perfectly.

CRANBERRY
Vaccinium oxycoccus

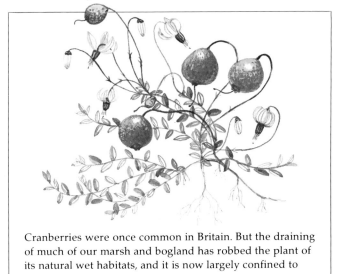

Cranberries were once common in Britain. But the draining of much of our marsh and bogland has robbed the plant of its natural wet habitats, and it is now largely confined to the north of England and Wales.

The berry of the wild plant, mottled red and ¼ inch (0.6 cm) across, is inedible raw, and you are unlikely to find enough for cooking. But it can be made into sauce like the larger American species. In fact, its origins, name and traditional uses are solidly British, and the fruit is mentioned (as 'fenberry') in a herbal published in 1578. Like so much else, cranberry recipes were preserved by British settlers in America, and only later brought back into use here.

COWBERRY
Vaccinium vitis-idaea

This little shrub is a close relative of the cranberry, and one of its names is in fact mountain cranberry. It grows to a maximum height of 12 inches (32 cm) on some moors in the northern parts of the British Isles.

Like cranberries, the red, spherical berries are sharp and scarcely edible when raw, though they make a good jelly. (They need some apple added for the pectin.)

Cowberry

CROWBERRY
Empetrum nigrum

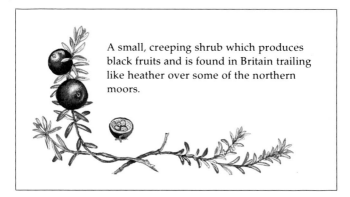

A small, creeping shrub which produces black fruits and is found in Britain trailing like heather over some of the northern moors.

The fruits are used in Arctic regions and probably have some value as a source of Vitamin C. Although it is difficult to gather the fruit in any quantity, some experimenters have enjoyed jelly made from it.

Primrose

Cowslip

COWSLIP
Primula veris

The cheerful, wobbly blossoms of the cowslip have made it
one of our favourite flowers, and it has probably suffered
more from overpicking than any other of our once-
common meadow flowers. Yet its name hardly suggests
such popularity. It is a euphemism for 'cowslop', no doubt
an indication of the plant's liking for mucky fields.

It was once widely used in kitchens, making one of the very best
country wines, and a curious 'vinegar' which was drunk with soda
water rather than being used as a condiment. (To show the devasta-
tion some of these recipes must have wreaked on flower popula-
tions, this particular recipe required two pints of cowslip blossoms
to make a pint and a half of vinegar.)

PRIMROSE
Primula vulgaris

The symbol of spring, with its pure, pale, delicately fragrant yellow flowers and crinkly leaves. The primrose can grow abundantly on chalk banks, railway embankments, shady woods, even on cliffs, but it is greatly reduced near big towns and cities.

Primrose blossoms have mostly been used in identical ways to cowslips, for making drinks, and as a dressing for roast veal.

LADY'S BEDSTRAW
Galium verum

Lady's bedstraw is a feathery, insubstantial plant, whose myriads of tiny yellow flowers smell of honey when cool and fresh. But when the plant is dried it develops the characteristic hay-like smell of coumarin (like woodruff, also a member of the bedstraw family).

Coumarin breaks down to yield a powerful anti-coagulant, dicoumarol, and there is always a small quantity of this in picked specimens of the plant. Yet lady's bedstraw must also contain some enzyme-like substance which overrides this, as it is of proven value as a styptic, and for curdling milk into junkets and cheese. I have never found full instructions for this old practice, and have not yet succeeded in making more than a thin skin of rather bitter junket with it. But experiment with different consistencies of milk, different temperatures and parts of the plant, and see if you can rediscover the recipe.

GOOSEGRASS, CLEAVERS
Galium aparine

> Widespread and abundant in hedges, woods and cultivated
> ground. A straggling annual, with whorls of 6 to 8 leaves,
> covered in all parts with tiny turned-down prickles.
> Flowers: inconspicuous, white, May–June.

A great children's plant, which clings mercilessly to trousers and
coats and any rough surface which brushes against it. If you look at a
section of the stalk of leaf under a microscope you will see that the
plant's sticking power is due to the hook-like bristles which cover
every part of it. Seen like this, they look positively dangerous, and
certainly not fit to eat. But look at the hooks again after the plant has
been plunged into boiling water for a few seconds, and you will see
that they have 'melted' and quite lost their forbidding sharpness.

Boiled as a spinach before the hard round seeds appear,
goosegrass makes tolerable eating, and can, moreover, be picked
through snow and frost when few other green plants are to be
found. John Evelyn recommends the young shoots in spring soups
and puddings.

Few plants can have had their various parts put to so many in-
genious uses. The seeds have been roasted and used as a coffee. In
green state they were used to adorn the tops of lacemakers' pins: the
young seeds were pushed on to the pins to make a sort of padded
head. And some books report that the prickly stems and leaves were
used to strain hair out of fresh milk.

WOODRUFF
Galium odoratum

> Widespread and often abundant in ancient woods and
> hedgebanks, especially beech, and on chalk and limestone.
> Flowers April to June, small, white and four-petalled, in
> loose heads. Grows in clusters to about 1 foot (30 cm) high,
> with whorls of six to nine leaves at intervals up the smooth
> stems.

In the late spring, the edges of beech woods are often thickly car-
peted with the young shoots of woodruff, immaculate in their tiny

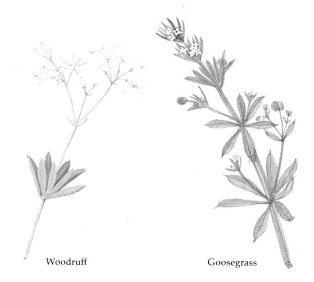

Woodruff   Goosegrass

marble-white flowers and brisk green ruffs. When they are green the plants are almost odourless; but allow them to dry and they quickly develop the cool, fresh smell of new-mown hay. Indeed, the plant was once popular for scenting dried linen and laying in beds.

This smell, which you will recognise if you have dried meadow-sweet or melilot, is due to a chemical called coumarin (see lady's bedstraw, p. 119). The scent readily transfers to liquids, and makes dried woodruff an ideal herb to add to summer wine cups. A bottle of pure apple juice in which a sprig has been allowed to steep for a week or so, becomes positively ambrosial.

The classic woodruff recipe is for Maibowl, traditionally drunk in Germany on May 1st. Steep a bunch of dried woodruff in a jug of Moselle wine. Add a couple of tablespoons of sugar dissolved in water. Chill, and serve with thinly sliced orange.

COMMON COMFREY
Symphytum officinale

Widespread and common in ditches and by river banks throughout the British Isles. Flowers June to October, white, cream, mauve or pink bells in clusters. The plant is a

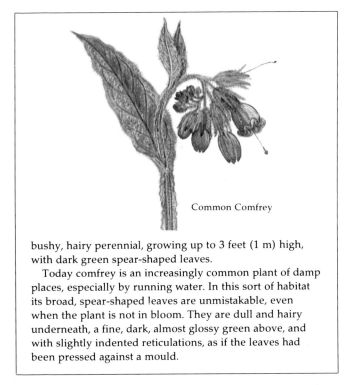

Common Comfrey

bushy, hairy perennial, growing up to 3 feet (1 m) high,
with dark green spear-shaped leaves.

Today comfrey is an increasingly common plant of damp
places, especially by running water. In this sort of habitat
its broad, spear-shaped leaves are unmistakable, even
when the plant is not in bloom. They are dull and hairy
underneath, a fine, dark, almost glossy green above, and
with slightly indented reticulations, as if the leaves had
been pressed against a mould.

It is the leaves which are now used in cookery. Don't worry about
their furriness; this disappears completely during cooking. Nor is
there much need to be particular about the age of the leaves you use,
for in my experience the older ones (provided of course they have
not started to wither) have more flavour than the younger. One way
of using them is to boil them like spinach, with plenty of seasoning.
There is no need to add butter, as the leaves themselves are fairly
glutinous.

The best recipe for comfrey leaves is a Teutonic fritter called
Schwarzwurz. Leave the stalks on the comfrey leaves, wash well, and
dip into a thin batter made from egg, flour and water. Then fry the
battered leaf in oil for not more than two minutes. For a more succulent result stick two or three similarly-sized leaves together before
battering. The crisp golden batter contrasts delightfully with the
mild, glutinous leaves.

The young leaf spears, picked in March when they are no more
than a couple of inches tall, make excellent salads, not unlike sliced
cucumber.

Comfrey (from the Latin *confervere*, to grow together) was the medieval herbalists' favourite bone-setter. The root was lifted in the spring, grated up and used as plaster is today. In a short while the mash would set as solid as a hard wood. In fact the whole plant was one of those 'wonder herbs' that was used for every sort of knitting operation from drawing splinters to healing ruptures.

Gerard's recommendation was even more eclectic:

The slimie substance of the roote made in a posset of ale, and given to drinke against the paine in the backe, gotten by any violent motion, as wrestling, or over much use of women, doth in fower or five daies perfectly cure the same. . . .

BORAGE
Borago officinalis

Quite common as an escape on waysides and waste places. Flowers: May to September, bright blue, with reflexed petals and prominent purple stamens. A loosely bushy annual, with conspicuously hairy stems, leaves and sepals.

Borage once had a great reputation as a sort of herbal pep-pill. It was renowned as an aphrodisiac and as a general dispeller of melancholy and depression. John Evelyn clearly understood the type of person who would perennially be in need of such aids when he wrote that 'the sprigs . . . are of known virtue to revive the hypochondriac and cheer the hard student'.

Whatever its medicinal qualities, the young leaves and bright blue, star-like flowers make a refreshing and fragrant addition to claret cups and other summer drinks, particularly in combination with woodruff. The star-shaped petals look appealing floated out on top of the drink – or frozen inside ice cubes. In more leisurely days, Richard Jeffries noted in *Nature Near London* (1883), borage leaves used 'to float in the claret cup ladelled out to thirsty travellers at the London railway stations'.

LUNGWORT
Pulmonaria officinalis

> An intriguing flower, somewhat similar to the closely
> related comfrey, except that its leaves are covered with a
> rash of white spots.

Lungwort is a frequent escape from gardens, where it used to be
grown as a medicine 'gainst the infirmities and ulcers of the lungs'.
Gerard also recommends it as a boiled vegetable.

OYSTER PLANT
Mertensia maritima

> A rare relative of the comfrey. The oyster plant grows on a
> few stretches of coastal shingle in Scotland, in prostrate
> mats.

Its fleshy leaves have been eaten both raw and cooked, and are said
to taste like oysters.

Lungwort   Oyster Plant

GROUND IVY
Glechoma hederacea

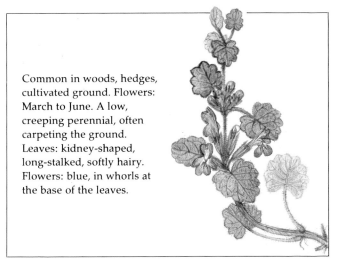

Common in woods, hedges, cultivated ground. Flowers: March to June. A low, creeping perennial, often carpeting the ground. Leaves: kidney-shaped, long-stalked, softly hairy. Flowers: blue, in whorls at the base of the leaves.

The dried leaves of ground ivy make one of the more agreeable herbal teas, cooling and with a sharp, slight fragrance.

Before hops became widely accepted in the seventeenth century, ground ivy – known then as alehoof – was one of the chief agents for flavouring and clarifying ale. Culpeper wrote of it: 'It is good to tun up with new drink, for it will clarify it in a night, that it will be fitter to be dranke the next morning; or if any drinke be thick with removing or any other accident, it will do the like in a few hours.'

BALM
Melissa officinalis

Another introduced herb, naturalised in a few places in the south of England. Balm is an undistinguished plant much like a bushy mint, yet it was very popular in Elizabethan gardens. Bees adore the flowers, and it was reputed that they would never leave a garden that had a clump of them growing. While a beehive was still a standard fixture in gardens, so was a bee-balm.

Balm

It was also grown for its lemon-scented leaves, which flavoured wines and teas. When lemons were scarce they were sometimes used to give a tang of apple jelly, and added to stuffings and salads.

WHITE DEAD-NETTLE
Lamium album

Widespread and common in hedgebanks, waste places, etc. Flowers March to September.

RED DEAD-NETTLE
Lamium purpureum

> Widespread and abundant in cultivated ground. Flowers throughout the year.

HENBIT
Lamium amplexicaule

> Locally common in cultivated ground. Flowers April to August.

YELLOW ARCHANGEL
Galeobdolon luteum

> Widespread and locally common in old woodland and shady hedgerows in England and Wales. Flowers May to June.

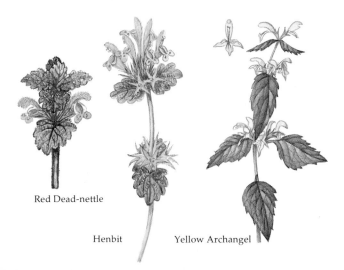

Red Dead-nettle

Henbit   Yellow Archangel

All the above members of the dead-nettle family can be used in a similar way to chickweed. The young tops and leaves can be added to salads, stir-fried as a green vegetable either by themselves or in company with other spring greens, and included, finely chopped, in *sauces vertes*.

WATER MINT
Mentha aquatica

Widespread and common by the edges of streams, in damp meadows, and woods, throughout the British Isles. Flowers July to September. A rough, hairy mint, often growing in quite sizeable clumps up to 2 feet (60 cm) high. The leaves are frequently tinged with purple, and grow in opposed pairs. Bluish-lilac flowers chiefly in a round bushy head at the top of the plant.

Water mint can be used exactly as if it were a garden mint. But if you should find its taste a little too bitter, even in a well-sugared mint sauce, try this recipe for Indian mint chutney, in which the wild mint's sharper qualities can be a positive virtue.

Wash and dry about 2 oz (50 gm) of mint leaves, and grind to a thick paste with a quarter of a cupful of vinegar. (A liquidiser will do the job just as well.) Chop up a quarter of a pound of tamarind (obtainable from most delicatessens), 2 oz (50 gm) green chillies (less if you do not like hot chutneys), a good-sized onion and a clove of garlic. Add these ingredients, plus a dessertspoonful of salt, to the mint paste and mix thoroughly. Bottle and store for a few days before using.

Alternatively, capitalise on the cool, sharp fragrance of water mint by adding a few sprigs to pots of China tea, or by making a mint julep. Wash a bunch of water mint, put it in a basin and bruise with the back of a spoon. Add one cup of brown sugar, one cup of pine-apple juice, and the juice of four lemons. Stir the mixture well and allow to stand for about four or five hours. Strain into a jug, and add three bottles of dry ginger, ice, some thin slices of lemon and a few sprigs of fresh mint.

There are over a dozen varieties of mint growing either wild or naturalised in Britain. All can be used more or less like water mint, though the quality of their flavours varies enormously. The following are the most frequently found:

CORN MINT
Mentha arvensis

Widespread and frequent in arable land, heaths, damp woodland rides.

A much-maligned plant whose fragrance has been described as 'acrid' by one writer, like 'wet mouldy gorgonzola' by Geoffrey Grigson, but as 'a strong fulsome mixed smell of mellow apples and gingerbread' by the eighteenth-century mint expert William Sole. You must judge for yourself.

SPEAR MINT
Mentha spicata

The mint usually grown in gardens, and frequently found naturalised near houses.

APPLE MINT
Mentha rotundifolia

An uncommon native in a few spots in the south-west,
otherwise a garden escape.

Apple-scented, and good in summer drinks.

WHORLED MINT
Mentha verticillata

Widespread and not uncommon in damp places. Many
members of the mint family hybridise readily with each
other, and this species is a cross between our two
commonest mints, *Mentha arvensis*, and *Mentha aquatica*.

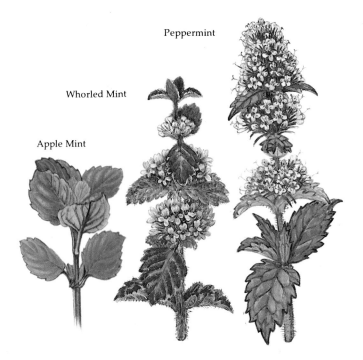

Peppermint

Whorled Mint

Apple Mint

PEPPERMINT
Mentha piperita

Uncommon in the south and west. This mint occurs only rarely in the wild, yet it is a natural hybrid between spear mint, *Mentha spicata*, and water mint, *Mentha aquatica*.

It was not discovered in this country until the late seventeenth century. But why *pepper*mint? It has a sharp taste, certainly, but nothing like the fieriness of pepper. The herb is now extensively cultivated for its aromatic oil, which is used in toothpastes, sweets, and indigestion remedies.

MARJORAM
Origanum vulgare

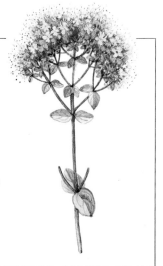

Widespread and locally common in grassy places on chalk and limestone. Rare in Scotland. Flowers July to October. A slender herb, growing up to 3 feet (90 cm) high, with downy stems extensively branched near the top of the plant. The leaves are oval and usually untoothed, and the flowers a pale, pinkish purple, in bunches at the head of the plant.

The marjoram which grows wild in this country is often known as oregano. It is spicier than sweet marjoram, *Origanum majorana*, but is still one of our most pleasantly fragrant herbs. In summer its flowers are alive with bees, who would appear to have a better opinion of our native herbs than us. We scarcely ever use the herb, but in the Mediterranean it is much valued as a flavouring for the more earthy, country dishes.

When you find marjoram growing wild on a dry heath or chalky roadside bank, its flimsy, slightly grey-tinted leaves look exceedingly appetising, and used raw they do indeed make a pleasantly pungent addition to salads. For use as a herb, pick some sprigs of the plant, flowers and all, whilst it is in full bloom. Later strip off the leaves and blossoms from the rather wiry stalk.

Wild marjoram is paramountly a meat herb. It gives a fine savour to stews and casseroles, to spaghetti sauces and shepherd's pie, even to grilled steaks, if they are first rubbed with the herb. But one of the most interesting recipes for the freshly picked plant is olives oregano. When olives are steeped in a marinade of flavoured oil, they acquire something of the aroma of the herb.

To one pound (450 gm) of pricked olives in a jar, add one cup of olive oil, one teaspoon of thyme, one teaspoon of crushed peppercorns, and three teaspoons of chopped wild marjoram. Close the jar, shake well and leave in a refrigerator for at least two days. Olives treated like this make a perfect centrepiece for a lunch for the season when marjoram is in flower. Serve them with a light red wine and cheese.

Wild marjoram becomes sweeter as it dries and can then be used in a wider range of dishes. One unusual recipe is for herb scones, to be served with roasted meat. Rub 2 oz (50 gm) of butter into 4 oz (100 gm) of salted flour. Add a heaped teaspoon of dried marjoram, and enough cold water to make a stiff dough. Mix well but lightly with a knife, and then shape into thin cakes with your hand. Put these on a greased tray in the oven for about quarter of an hour (longer if you are cooking the meat slowly).

WILD THYME
Thymus drucei

Widespread and often abundant in grassy places, especially on chalk and limestone, and on sandy heaths. Flowers June to August. A prostrate, creeping plant, with rather woody stems and runners. Leaves very small, oval, and ranged in many opposing pairs along the stalks. The flowers are reddish purple in roundish bunches at the ends of the stalks.

Wild thyme is a herb growing abundantly in open places. But be under no illusions: your nostrils are not going to be filled with that heady aroma as you stride over the springy turf with your basket. Wild thyme has neither the bushy forthrightness nor the pungency of cultivated thyme, *Thymus vulgaris*. It is a subtle, skulking plant, often growing entirely below grass level. Finding it is a hands-and-knees job, a rummage through the miniature downland flora, the milkworts and violets, for a sprig of toy, oval leaves that yield that clovy smell between the fingers. Then, tracing the runners back, following their meanderings through the dry lower stems of the grasses back to the woody root.

For a short while, when each plant is in flower, picking is a simpler exercise – though less rewarding I think than the inch-by-inch ferreting for the spring and autumn shoots. The flower heads are large compared to the size of the plant, and like marjoram conspicuous for their attendant insects. Wild thyme is best picked when in full bloom, so that the honey-scented flowers can be used as well as the leaves.

If you like you can strip the leaves and flowers off the stalk before using. But as wild thyme is considerably milder than the garden variety you can afford to use large sprigs of it liberally – and indeed to try it out in unconventional combinations. The great virtue of wild thyme is precisely its versatility.

Try it as a tea, or chopped finely and beaten into butter. Add it to omelettes and to stuffings for roast chicken. But think of it, too, as a convenient way of perking up picnic or outdoor food. A few sprigs can be added to pots of cottage cheese, tucked inside sandwiches, thrown into almost any casserole and wrapped up with roast joints in foil. In Scandinavia, steeped in aquavit, it makes one of the favourite varieties of schnapps.

BROOKLIME
Veronica beccabunga

Widespread and common by the edges of streams and in wet places. Flowers May to September.

A quite widely used salad plant in Northern Europe, rather bitter. The American species was praised by *Scientific American* as 'a salad plant equal to the watercress. Delightful in flavour, healthful and anti-scorbutic.'

RAT'S-TAIL PLANTAIN
Plantago major

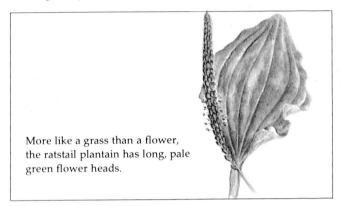

More like a grass than a flower, the ratstail plantain has long, pale green flower heads.

Plantain is one of those plants that positively thrive on rough treatment. The more you walk on it or mow it the better it thrives. The North American Indians went as far as to call it 'English Man's Foot', for wherever the white man walked and worked, plantain followed. Its rosettes of ribbed oval leaves are abundant on lawns and footpaths.

The young leaves have been used as a salad herb, but I find them too tough and bitter when raw, and would advise them to be well cooked as a spinach.

RED VALERIAN
Centranthus ruber

A perennial, with small red, pink or white flowers.

In France and Italy the very young leaves of this plant are sometimes boiled with butter as greens, or eaten raw in salads – though they are rather bitter used this way.

Cornsalad

Red Valerian

Red valerian was introduced to Britain from Southern Europe in the sixteenth century, and was a great favourite of Gerard's, though he ascribed no practical uses for the plant. Its red flowers now adorn many stony and rocky places in the south-west.

CORNSALAD
Valerianella locusta

Quite common in arable ground, on banks and walls.
Flowers April to July.

A diminutive and rather bland plant that is nevertheless a useful addition to salads, especially as it stays in leaf for most of the winter. It – and its cultivated cousins – are more popular in France, where they are known as *'mache'* and *'salade de prêtre'*. The leaves are best served with a sharp dressing to bring out their flavour and texture.

COMMON CHAMOMILE
Chamaemelum nobile

Common chamomile is not common at all; in fact it is a rather rare plant of grassy and heathy places in the south of England. It has a daisy-like flower and feathery leaves, but being a member of the huge and complex *compositae* family this is scarcely enough to identify it. It can be told from the very similar scentless mayweed and corn chamomile by an absence of down beneath its leaves. But its most conspicuous characteristic is its sweet apple scent, for which it was once much valued in rockeries, and even planted on lawns instead of grass.

Chamomile is still cultivated on a small scale for its flower-heads, which make a fine herbal tea. The heads are gathered when the petals just begin to turn down, and are used either fresh or dried.

YARROW
Achillea millefolium

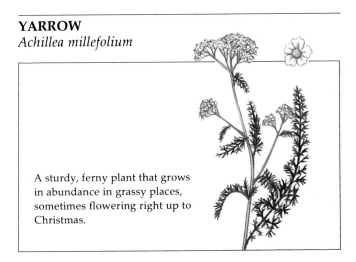

A sturdy, ferny plant that grows in abundance in grassy places, sometimes flowering right up to Christmas.

Yarrow had a great reputation amongst herbalists as an astringent for wounds. Used in small quantities it can make a cool if rather bitter addition to salads. It can also be used as a cooked vegetable by removing the feathery leaves from the tough stems, boiling for ten minutes, straining off the water, and then simmering in butter.

WORMWOOD
Artemisia absinthium

A strongly scented perennial with yellowish flower-heads from July to August.

A bitter oil extracted from the flower-heads of this attractive silky-grey plant is the key ingredient of absinthe, that most potent of alcoholic drinks. The flowers have also been used on the Continent to counteract the greasiness of goose and duck dishes. Used in small quantities the herb has beneficial, tonic properties. But in excess it can be damaging to the heart. It also contains an anthelmintic (worm-dispeller) called santonin, which is a hallucinogen if taken in overdose. Objects first appear blue and then change to yellow.

MUGWORT
Artemisia vulgaris

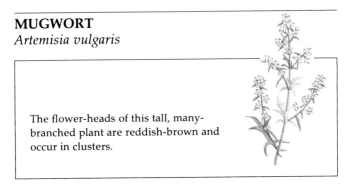

The flower-heads of this tall, many-branched plant are reddish-brown and occur in clusters.

A common native relative of wormwood, whose bitter leaves have been used to flavour beer, and dried, as in tea.

OX-EYE DAISY
Chrysanthemum leucanthemum

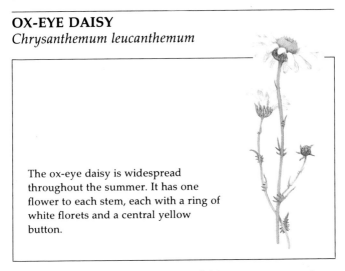

The ox-eye daisy is widespread throughout the summer. It has one flower to each stem, each with a ring of white florets and a central yellow button.

John Evelyn reported that the roots of this, our commonest large daisy, were eaten as a salad vegetable in Spain.

TANSY
Chrysanthemum vulgare

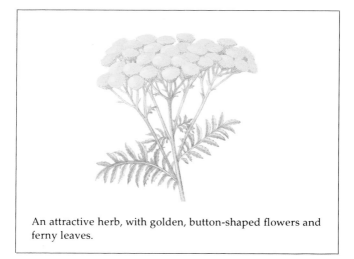

An attractive herb, with golden, button-shaped flowers and ferny leaves.

There was a time when tansy was one of the most widely grown garden herb. It was a key item in the housewife's armoury of medicines, and had an extraordinarily wide range or uses in the kitchen.

At Easter the young leaves were traditionally served with fried eggs and used to flavour puddings made from milk, flour and eggs. This may have been to symbolise the bitter herbs eaten by the Jews at Passover, though one sixteenth-century writer explained that it was to counteract the effects 'engendered of Fish in the Lent season'. He may have been on to something, as the quality of fish at that time no doubt encouraged the development of parasitic worms, and Oil of Tansy is quite effective as a vermifuge.

Earlier still, the juice was extracted from the chopped leaves and used to flavour omelettes. This gave the name 'Tansye' in the fifteenth century as a generic term for any herb-flavoured omelette. And there was a delightful medieval bubble-and-squeak, made from a fry-up of tansy leaves, green corn and violets, and served with orange and sugar.

But it must be said that tansy is not very tempting to modern palates. It smells like linament and has a hot, bitter taste. Moreover it can be a dangerous irritant to the stomach if taken in excess. But try it for yourself. Whatever you think of its flavour it is an attractive herb, with its golden, button-shaped flowers and ferny leaves.

MILK THISTLE
Silybum marianum

Centuries ago this handsome thistle was introduced into Western European gardens from the Mediterranean, for use as a pot-herb. It is a distinctive plant, growing up to 6 feet (150 cm) high, and its spiny leaves are intricately veined in white.

Almost all parts of the plant were eaten. The leaves were trimmed of prickles and boiled. The stems were peeled, soaked in water to remove the bitterness and then stewed like rhubarb. Even the spiny bracts that surround the broad flower-head were eaten like globe artichokes.

Milk thistle is widespread but only locally common in the British Isles. It is liable to spring up in any waste place, but prefers areas near the sea, and especially the Thames Estuary.

MARSH THISTLE
Cirsium palustre

A tall, common thistle of grassy places and woods, especially on wet ground.

The young shoots have been used like burdock in some European countries. The prickles and the tough outer peel are removed, and the stalks then used in salads or boiled.

BURDOCK
Arctium minus

Widespread and common throughout the British Isles, at the edges of woods, and on roadsides and waste ground. Flowers July to September. A stiff, bushy plant, up to 3 feet (90 cm) high, conspicuous early in the year for its large, floppy, heart-shaped leaves, and later for its stout branching stems. The flower-heads are egg-shaped and thistle-like, and turn at the fruiting stage into the well-known prickly burs.

Milk Thistle

Marsh Thistle

Burdock

Burdock is often mistaken for rhubarb. Often there is nothing to be seen of the plant except its huge leaves draped over the ground. The parts to pick are the young leaf stems which begin to sprout round about May (after September they are too tough and stringy). The stems should be cut into 2 inch (5 cm) lengths and the hard outer peel stripped off. This will leave you with a moist core about the thickness of a pipe-cleaner. This can be chopped and used raw in salads, boiled and served with butter like asparagus, or added to meat soups. It has a flavour slightly reminiscent of new potatoes.

Burdock roots are used quite extensively in Japanese cooking. They are sliced thinly and braised with soy sauce, or wrapped in their own leaves and silver foil and roasted whole.

HARDHEAD, LESSER KNAPWEED
Centaurea nigra

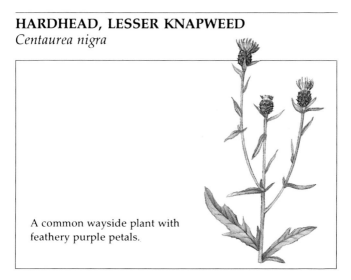

A common wayside plant with feathery purple petals.

The petals may be used in salads and give a splash of unusual colour if scattered over a greenleaf base.

SALSIFY
Tragopogon porrifolius

Salsify still grows wild in a few places, chiefly near estuaries in the south-east of England. It is a tall, straight plant, with purplish dandelion-like flowers.

Although picking the wild specimens is not to be encouraged whilst the plant is still so uncommon, it ought to be purchased more often from the few greengrocers which stock the cultivated variety. The long white roots are first carefully peeled, and then boiled or steamed with butter and lemon juice. The flavour is sufficiently individual for the roots to be served as a dish on their own.

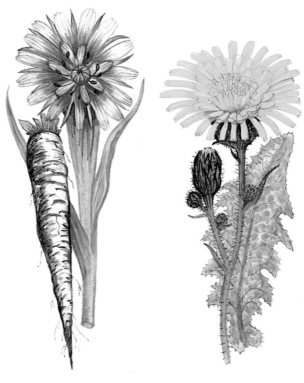

Salsify   Corn Sow-thistle

The following four members of the daisy family can all have their leaves used in salads, as dandelions:

CORN SOW-THISTLE
Sonchus arvensis

Widespread and common throughout the British Isles, on road verges and cultivated ground. Flowers July to October.

CHICORY
Cichorium intybus

Widespread throughout England and Wales, but only
locally common, usually in grassy and waste places on
chalk. Flowers June to September.

The 'succory' of the old herbalists, a tall, distinguished plant with
startling cornflower-blue blossoms. Chicory is probably not a
native of the British Isles, but it still grows in quite a wide range of
grassy habitats, especially on chalk and limestone.

The roots are boiled and eaten by the Arabs, and it is from the
Arabic *Chicouryeh* that the English name for the plant is derived.
Roast and ground, the roots make an acceptable (though slightly
bitter) substitute for, or addition to, coffee, and have been
extensively cultivated for this purpose.

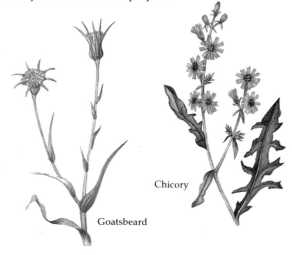

Chicory

Goatsbeard

GOATSBEARD
Tragopogon pratensis

Widespread and common in dry, grassy places. Flowers:
June to September.

The young flower-buds can be added to salads or stir-fried.

NIPPLEWORT
Lapsana communis

Widespread and common on
shady banks, roadsides, etc.
Flowers from June to
September.

DANDELION
Taraxacum officinale

Widespread and abundant in
open and grassy places
throughout British Isles.
Flowers February to
November, but especially
April and May. Largish
golden-yellow flowers made
up of numerous fine petals,
on hollow stems up to 1 foot
(30 cm) tall. Leaves grow
from base of plant and are
roughly toothed. The whole
plant exudes a milky juice
when cut.

The dandelion is one of the most profuse of British weeds, and in
late spring is liable to cover almost any grassy place with its blazing
yellow flowers. Its leaves – and consequently its roots – can be
found at almost any time of the year except the very coldest, which

is welcome, given the wide range of food uses to which the plant can be put.

The normal use of the long white roots is to make a coffee substitute, which is almost indistinguishable from real coffee, yet which lacks the possibly injurious stimulant, caffeine. Dig up the roots in the autumn, when they are at their fattest and most mellow, and scrub well (though do not peel). Dry them thoroughly, preferably in the sun, and then roast in an oven until they are brittle. Grind them fairly coarsely and use as ordinary coffee.

The Japanese use the root as a vegetable, cooked Nituke-style. Chop the scrubbed roots into thin rings. Sauté these in vegetable oil, using about one tablespoonful of oil to one cup of chopped roots. Then add a small amount of water, a little salt, and cover the pan. Stew until the roots are soft and most of the moisture and added water have evaporated. Finally add a dash of soya sauce.

It is especially useful as a salad plant, since the leaves can be gathered at almost any time of the year. Only after prolonged frost or snow is it impossible to find any. Choose the youngest leaves and strip them from the plant by hand. The root is quite strong enough to be unaffected by this sort of picking. (If you have dandelions growing in your garden, try manuring them and covering the lower parts of the leaves with earth or a cardboard tube to blanch them like chicory. They did this in medieval gardens and produced gigantic plants as a result.)

When you have sufficient leaves, trim off any excess stalk, and wash well. The roughly chopped leaves can be made into a good salad simply by dressing with olive oil, lemon juice and a trace of garlic. They can also be served in sandwiches with a dash of Worcester sauce, or cooked with butter like spinach.

Pissenlit au lard is a dandelion dish sometimes served in French restaurants. It consists of small pieces of crispy fried bacon, served hot on a raw dandelion salad base, and dressed with vinegar, bacon fat and seasoning. For extra colour and a new texture, throw in a few of the flower-heads as well.

The nineteenth-century French chef Marcel Boulestin recommended a salad made from equal quantities of dandelion 'hearts' (unopened flower-buds plus young surrounding leaves) and chopped beetroot. The French name, and some of the local English names, should warn you that the plant has a small reputation as a diuretic.

CATSEAR
Hypochoeris radicata

Common in dry pastures, open woods and other grassy places. Flowers May to September, but the leaves continue to grow through much of the winter.

Use young leaves as dandelion, in salad. Rough hawkbit (below) can be used in an identical fashion.

ROUGH HAWKBIT
Leontodon hispidus

Common in meadows, roadside verges and dry, grassy places. Flowers May to September.

Catsear   Rough Hawkbit

SAND LEEK
Allium scorodoprasum

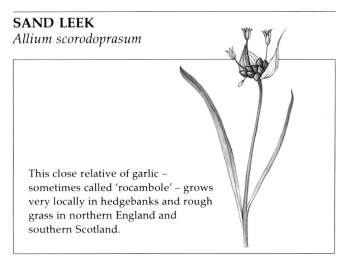

This close relative of garlic –
sometimes called 'rocambole' – grows
very locally in hedgebanks and rough
grass in northern England and
southern Scotland.

The plant has occasionally been taken into cultivation, or gathered
in the wild state, and the bulbs and stems used in the same way as
garlic.

CHIVES
Allium schoenoprasum

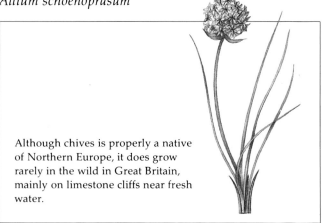

Although chives is properly a native
of Northern Europe, it does grow
rarely in the wild in Great Britain,
mainly on limestone cliffs near fresh
water.

Chives has long been cultivated as a herb, being especially prized
by those who like the characteristic flavour of onions, but only in

moderation. Its mildness and almost complete absence of a bulb have earned chives the name of 'Infant Onion'.

It is a highly adaptable herb, going well with cream cheese, potatoes, cucumber, salads and omelettes.

RAMSONS, WILD GARLIC
Allium ursinum

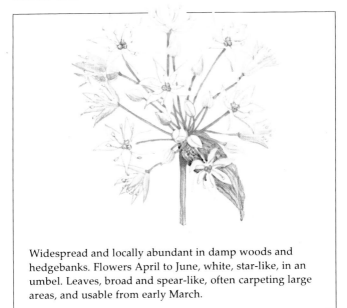

Widespread and locally abundant in damp woods and hedgebanks. Flowers April to June, white, star-like, in an umbel. Leaves, broad and spear-like, often carpeting large areas, and usable from early March.

Large colonies of ramsons can often be smelt tens of yards away, and garlic woods sometimes figured as landmarks in old land charters. But the taste and smell of small quantities of the leaf are milder than you would expect, and it makes an excellent substitute for garlic or spring onion in salads. One experimenter recommends the leaves added to peanut butter sandwiches.

Try the leaves chopped in sour cream or mayonnaise. Or take advantage of their size and cut them into long, thin strips to lay criss-cross over sliced tomatoes.

Three-cornered leek, *Allium triquetrum*, quite commonly naturalised in the south-west; and crow garlic, *Allium vineale*, common in arable fields and waysides – can both be used as ramsons, or as a coarse chives.

BATH ASPARAGUS,
SPIKED STAR OF BETHLEHEM
Ornithogalum pyrenaicum

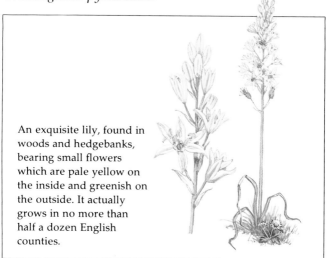

An exquisite lily, found in
woods and hedgebanks,
bearing small flowers
which are pale yellow on
the inside and greenish on
the outside. It actually
grows in no more than
half a dozen English
counties.

While the flowers are still in bud in May, bunches of the plant were
picked around Bristol and Bath, and sold to be eaten like asparagus.

ASPARAGUS
Asparagus officinalis

There are two varieties of asparagus growing wild in this
country. *Asparagus officinalis* ssp. *prostratus*, the prostrate,
native subspecies, and ssp. *officinalis*, the introduced garden
variety which is now naturalised in the wild in a few
places. Distinctive red berries appear on this plant from
April to June. Flowers greenish yellow.

Neither type grows as sumptuously as cultivated specimens, and
both are uncommon. So picking is not really to be recommended.
The part of both plants which is eaten is the fat shoot, or 'spear',
which grows from the rootstock in early summer.

Asparagus

LORDS AND LADIES, ARUM LILY
Arum maculatum   **POISONOUS**

A plant most country children are wisely taught to beware of. It grows abundantly in the shade of hedgerows and woods, like so many painted china ornaments. It is a plant which appears in several deceptively attractive disguises. The glossy, arrow-shaped leaves are amongst the very first foliage to appear in late winter. They are followed by a paler green cowl, which encloses the club-shaped flower. In late summer the hood withers and the flower produces a spike of shiny orange berries.

All these stages and parts produce in the raw state an acrid, burning juice, which is a serious irritant both internally and externally. The root also contains this poisonous element; yet if it is well baked it is completely harmless. The cooked and ground roots were once in demand in this country under the name Portland sago, since the trade was centred round the Isle of Portland. The powder was used like Salop or as a substitute for arrowroot.

EARLY PURPLE ORCHIS
Orchis mascula

The pink or purple flowers of the early purple orchis appear in April.

It would be criminal to dig up any of the dwindling colonies of British orchids, let alone for food. Yet this lilac-flowered woodland species deserves a place for completeness' sake, as it has been one of the more fascinating and valuable of wild foods. The tubers contain a starch-like substance called bassorine, which has in it more nutritive matter than any other single plant product, one ounce being sufficient to sustain a person for a whole day.

In the Middle East, where the plant is more common, it is still widely used. The roots are dug up after the plant has flowered, and are occasionally eaten as they stand, either raw or cooked. But they are most usually made into a drink called Cahlab. For this the tubers are dried in the sun and ground into a rough flour. This is mixed with honey and cinnamon, and stirred into hot milk until it thickens.

In Britain, a similar drink called Salop was a common soft drink long before the introduction of coffee houses. In Victorian books it is mentioned as a tea-break beverage of manual workers. They made it with water more often than with milk, sometimes lacing it with spirits, sometimes brewing it so thick that it had to be eaten with a spoon.

REED
Phragmites australis

This is the common reed which so readily forms dense beds in still, shallow water.

When the stalks are still green it often happens that they are punctured or broken in some way. When this happens a sugary substance slowly exudes and hardens into a gum. The North American Indians used to collect this and break it into balls which they ate as sweets. Another Indian way of preparing a sweet from the plant was to cut the reeds when still green, dry them, grind them and sift out the flour. This contains so much sugar that when it is placed near a fire it swells, browns, and is eaten like toasted marshmallow.

DITTANDER
Lepidium latifolium

Between July and September a cluster of white flowers
appears on this extremely robust plant.

Dittander has a hot, pungent root, and was gathered from the wild
and occasionally grown in gardens as a condiment before horseradish and pepper became popular. It is a perennial and has an
obstinate and aggressive root system like horseradish, yet is now
uncommon in the wild. Only beside a few estuaries on the south
and east coasts can the tall, elegant leaves still be found.

SEAWEEDS

Although they reproduce by spores, not flowers and seeds, sea-weeds have seasons of growth like other plants. They produce shoots in the spring, grow quickly and luxuriantly during the summer, and wither in the winter. The best months to gather most seaweeds are May and June.

Seaweeds obtain their food entirely from the surrounding sea water and do not have roots in the conventional sense. However, they do have hold-fasts, by which they attach themselves to rocks and stones, and from which the stem-like part, or stipe, grows. The weed itself can regenerate from a cut stipe, provided the cut is not too near the hold-fast. So if you are cutting seaweed rather than gathering leaves which have been washed free of their moorings, leave plenty of stipe so that the weed can grow again.

Before cooking any seaweed always wash thoroughly in fresh water to remove sand, shells and other shoreline debris which may have stuck to it.

SOME COOKING HINTS

There are a number of basic ways of cooking all seaweeds. Slice them very thin and serve raw as a salad. A Chinese-style dressing of soy sauce, vinegar and a little sugar is a good accompaniment. Slice them a little less thinly, and stir-fry in sesame or sunflower oil for about 5 minutes – or in more oil at a higher temperature, until they are crisp on the outside. (Crisp-fried seaweeds are popular Chinese appetisers.)

Add larger pieces to soups and stews to thicken them. Most sea-weeds contain alginates – a kind of vegetable gelatine – which are released during prolonged cooking.

Seaweeds are low in calories but rich in minerals, particularly iodides, and you may take a little while to get used to their flavours. But do give them a fair chance; they are intriguing foods, and undeserving of their somewhat freakish reputation.

SEA LETTUCE
Ulva lactuca

Quite common on all types of shore, attached to stones and rocks, sea lettuce is especially fond of places where water runs into the sea.

DABBERLOCKS
Alaria esculenta

Commonest on exposed shores, where it takes the place of *Laminaria digitata*.

Enteromorpha intestinalis

Abundant on salt marshes and in dikes and rocky pools. A weed which should be picked in the early spring.

Dabberlocks   Kelp

Enteromorpha intestinalis

KELP
Laminaria digitata

Grows at the low-water mark on rocky shores all round the coast.

As well as a salad vegetable, is used as a source of alginates.

OARWEED
Laminaria saccharina

Often found attached to small stones on muddy and sandy flats.

The young stipes of this weed used to be sold in Scotland under the name of 'tangle'. One writer describes their taste as resembling that of peanuts.

A composite jelly, made from this weed and dulse and called *Pain des Algues*, used to be prepared on the coast of Armorica.

BLADDER WRACK
Fucus vesiculosus

Abundant on the middle shore, and unmistakable for its inflated bladders.

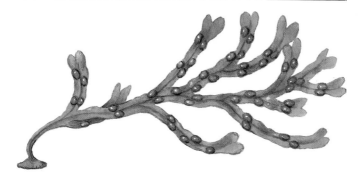

DULSE
Rhodymenia palmata

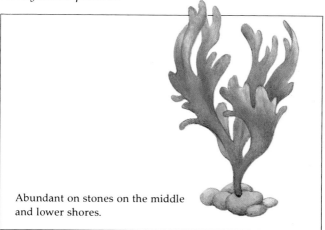

Abundant on stones on the middle and lower shores.

Dulse has been eaten raw as a salad, and in New England the dried fronds are used as a relish.

LAVER
Porphyra umbilicalis

Common all round Britain, especially on exposed shores on the west coast. Grows on rock and stones at most levels of the beach, especially where the stones are likely to be covered with sand. The fronds are thin, irregularly-shaped purple membranes.

In the south-west of Wales laver is considered a great delicacy, and it sells briskly in many food shops to those who don't want the bother of gathering it for themselves.

Yet it is one of the easier seaweeds to find and recognise, its translucent purple fronds liable to crop up on almost all levels of the shore. In Japan it is cultivated. Bundles of bamboo are placed on the sea bottom, just offshore, and transferred to fresh river water once the weed has established itself. In these conditions the laver apparently grows softer and more extensive fronds. The Chinese and Japanese make very varied use of their laver, in soups and stews, as a covering round rice balls, and in pickles and preserves.

In Britain there have been two classic, traditional uses: laver sauce for mutton, and laverbread. The first stage in any laver recipe is to reduce the weed to a sort of rough purée. First wash it well and then simmer in a little water until it is like well-cooked spinach. This is best done in a double saucepan as the laver sticks easily. This mush, if transferred to a jar, will keep well for several days.

It is this purée which is sold in Wales under the name of laverbread. It ends up in the place you would least expect it, on the breakfast table, rolled in oatmeal and fried in bacon fat.

To make laver sauce, beat up two cupfuls of the purée with an ounce (28 gm) of butter and the juice of one Seville orange.

PEPPER DULSE
Laurencia pinnatifida

An infrequent weed which forms dense tufts in rock crevices on the middle shore.

Pepper dulse is very pungent and is usually used as a condiment. In Iceland it has been employed as a substitute for chewing tobacco.

CARRAGHEEN, IRISH MOSS
Chondrus crispus

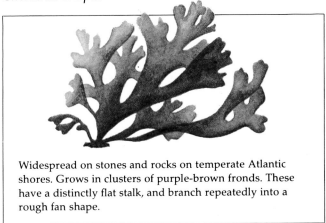

Widespread on stones and rocks on temperate Atlantic shores. Grows in clusters of purple-brown fronds. These have a distinctly flat stalk, and branch repeatedly into a rough fan shape.

Carragheen is an important source of alginates – vegetable gelatines which are used for thickening soups, emulsifying ice-creams and setting jellies. They can also be made into thin, durable films for use as edible sausage skins.

You can find carragheen on almost any western or southern shore. It is best gathered young, in April or May, and either used immediately or carefully dried. To use the weed fresh, wash it well, add one cup of weed to three cups of milk or water and sugar and flavouring to taste. Then simmer slowly until most of the weed has dissolved. Remove any undissolved fragments and pour into a mould to set. This produces a basic Irish moss blancmange or jelly, depending on whether you use milk or water. Ginger is good as a flavouring, and can be added in the form of the chopped root during the simmering of the weed.

To dry the weed, wash it well, and then lay out to dry on a wind-free surface out-of-doors. Wash it from time to time with fresh water, or simply leave it in the rain. After a while it will become bleached to a creamy-white colour. Trim off any tough stalks, dry thoroughly indoors, and then store in bags. The dried weed can be used exactly as if it were fresh.

Carragheen grows abundantly in the Channel Islands and during the war it was gathered and sold in shops. The demand was so great that boats had to be used in spite of the large number of mines in the area. The weed was used to thicken soups and stews.

Gigartina stellata

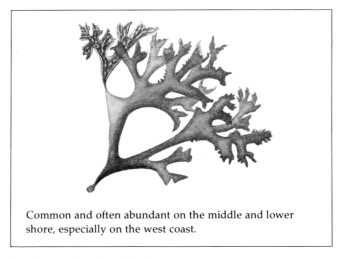

Common and often abundant on the middle and lower shore, especially on the west coast.

Can be used to make a jelly base.

The remaining three entries are not seaweeds, but being non-flowering plants fit more satisfactorily into this section than anywhere else.

MAIDENHAIR FERN
Adiantum capillis-veneris

A rare and delicate fern which grows on sheltered limestone cliffs in a few localities in the west.

In the eighteenth and nineteenth centuries it was used as a garnish to sweet dishes. Later it formed the basis of *capillaire*, which was a popular flavouring at the turn of the century. The fern (imported from Iceland) was simmered in water for several hours, and the liquid made into a thick syrup with sugar and orange-water. *Capillaire* was mixed with fruit juice and water to form soft drinks.

ICELAND MOSS
Cetraria islandica

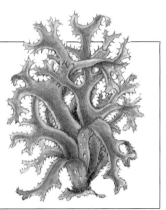

This rust-brown lichen grows amongst the heather and other ground plants on moorlands in Scotland and the north of England.

An edible jelly is sometimes made by boiling the plant, which is first soaked in water to remove the bitter flavour.

ROCK TRIPE
Umblicaria pustulata

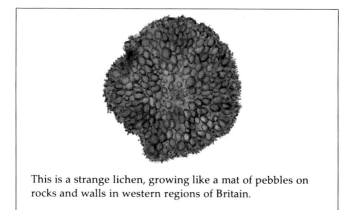

This is a strange lichen, growing like a mat of pebbles on rocks and walls in western regions of Britain.

It is edible if cooked like a seaweed, and some Arctic explorers have survived off it for weeks on end. Yet they have more praise for its powers of nourishment than for its taste; one gives the rather forbidding description 'a little like tapioca with a slight flavouring of liquorice'.

FUNGI

Wild fungi are the most misunderstood and maligned of all wild foods. There are 3000 species of large-bodied fungi growing in the British Isles, yet only twenty-odd of these are seriously poisonous. Admittedly, many hundreds of the remainder are inedible because of toughness, indigestibility or taste. But this scarcely seems sufficient to explain the blackening of the reputation of a whole biological category. Robert Graves has suggested that our hostility towards fungi may be a hangover from the time when there were religious taboos against their use by any persons outside the priesthood. I would guess that there are more down-to-earth reasons than this. It would be foolish to pretend that the identification of fungi is as easy as the identification of flowering plants. They have fewer differentiating characteristics, and even within one species can vary enormously, in shape, size and colour. Even though the number of poisonous species is comparatively very small, each one resembles maybe half a dozen edible types.

The *un*earthly qualities of fungi no doubt exaggerate these worries. They rise up quickly, in lightless places. Many of them thrive on the dead or dying remains of other plants – or worse, of animals. Their shapes can bear resemblances to other organisms, to corals, brains, ears and sexual parts.

But there is no doubt that much of the discomfort we feel about fungi is conditioned by culture and fashion. We do, after all, consume vast quantities of cultivated mushrooms. So the characteristic fungoid taste is not in itself repugnant. And in other parts of the world – in China, Scandinavia, Mediterranean Europe and Canada, for example – there is still extensive use of wild fungi.

At the famous fungi market in Munich over 300 edible species are licensed to be sold. In Russia the authorities issue cheap permits for the national conifer forests, where enormous quantities of fungi (mainly *Lactarius deliciosus*) are gathered for drying for the winter.

There are over a hundred quite edible species growing in this country and it is sad that so many of them go to waste. They have no especial food value (though they contain more protein than vegetables and considerable quantities of Vitamin D) but some intriguing tastes and textures, and are worthwhile trying for these alone.

There are no general rules about when and where fungi may be found. They grow in all sorts of environments at all times of the year. But there are some guidelines which can be deduced from the way that fungi grow. Fungi are characterised as a class by the fact that they do not contain any chlorophyll, and are thus unable to manufacture their own carbohydrates. They must live off those manufactured by other plants, either living or dead. Any ground which is rich in root structure or newly decaying plant litter is potentially good as a fungus bed. Mature woodlands and well-established pasture are both ideal environments. The more these host environments flourish, die, regenerate, the better off will be their attendant fungi. So although fungi have no use for direct light, they do prosper in areas where the underground growth and cycling of their hosts is stimulated by light: hedges, woodland clearings and paths, etc. They also like warmth and damp, and a year which begins with a long, fine summer, and continues with a wet, mild autumn, is likely to be as good for fungi as it is for other types of fruit. It is the right balance of sunlight, moisture and warmth which seems to be crucial. In wet summers fungi tend to appear more in woodland clearings; in dry summers in the shady, moisture-retaining spots. Some fungi appear in the spring and others can live through the winter. But the greatest number appear in the late summer and disappear with the first hard frosts.

SOME PICKING RULES

The following are a few suggestions about picking and preparation which apply to all fungi, and which will help guarantee you have good specimens this season, and more to come back to next.

1 Only pick those which satisfy *all* the specifications about size, colour, time of year and environment that are given on the following pages. These have been chosen so that it is very difficult to make a mistake if you follow them to the letter.

2 Don't pick specimens which are so old that they have started to decay, or so young that they have not yet developed their identifying characteristics.

3 Avoid gathering on very wet days; many fungi are highly porous, and a blewit, for instance, can soak up its own weight of water in a few hours. Moisture not only spoils the taste and texture but creates conditions where decomposition can proceed more quickly.

4 Don't cut fungi with a knife, or yank them out of the ground, either. You will need the whole stalk, and any sheath (or 'volva') for a full identification. The fungi we pick are simply the fruit bodies of the fungus plant proper, which is a complex net of fine threads called the mycelium growing around the roots, dead leaves, or whatever is the food source of the fungus. If this is broken by too careless picking, the plant can be damaged. The best way of picking a fungus is to twist it gently until it breaks free.

It is best to cut the earthy part of the stipe away *before* putting the mushroom into a basket. This will prevent it soiling those mushrooms already gathered, and will give a fair idea whether any maggots or insects have got into the cap via the stem. (The colour at the base of the stipe is also a valuable help to recognition in some species, e.g. the yellow-staining mushroom, p. 199.)

5 Gather your crop into an open, well-ventilated basket, not your pockets or a polythene bag. Fungi decay very quickly, and heat, congestion and stale air accelerate this process.

6 Go through all your specimens again carefully before cooking. Check their identification and discard any you are not confident about. Indigestion brought on by uncertainty about whether you have done yourself in can be just as uncomfortable as real food poisoning. Remember there are no infallible tricks with sixpences or salt which can identify all poisonous species.

7 To be especially careful cut each fungus in half and throw away any that are maggot-ridden or possessed of suspicious white gills (most of the deadly *Amanitas* have these). Also cut away decaying or wet pieces.

8 Clean the fungi before cooking. But there is no need to wash them or peel them, unless it is specifically stated in the text. Use them within 24 hours of picking.

9 In common with other new foods it is as well to try a fairly small portion the first time you eat any species. It is just possible that it may 'disagree with you'.

Having prepared your fungi, remember that there are many other ways of using them beyond the recipes given here for individual species.

Drying is a useful way of preserving them for the winter. Special fungi drying trays and small ovens are now available commercially, but to do the operation more cheaply, simply cut prepared specimens into slices about 2 mm thick and keep in a warm place or a dry currrent of air. Threading the slices (or the whole caps of smaller specimens) on to a string is a convenient and attractive way of doing this. They are dry when they feel crisp to the fingers and can be easily crumbled into small pieces. The fungi can be reconstituted by boiling in water for about twenty minutes.

Fungi can also be pickled by being simmered in water for about ten minutes, drained and put in jars under ordinary pickling vinegar.

All edible fungi can be made into soup, using the recipe on p. 194, or ketchup (p. 201). There is also scope for a whole new range of recipes based on a view of them as fruits rather than savouries. Try them stewed with sugar, like plums, or added to cakes and puddings, as if they were currants.

Finally, find out if your local natural history society or wildlife trust hold fungus forays in the autumn. These traditional foraging expeditions are now being revived all over the country, and there is no better way of getting to know the situations in which the different species grow, and how to look out for their identifying characteristics.

MOREL
Morchella esculenta

Not uncommon in sandy woods, waste ground and rubbish heaps, especially over chalky soils. Unusual in appearing from March to May. The cap is wrinkled like a coarse sponge, 2 to 3 inches (5 to 8 cm) across, greyish brown. Stem: white, hollow with no ring.

Morels are one of the most distinctive of fungi, and amongst the best to eat. They have an affinity with burnt places, and there are records of colonies springing up on bomb sites during the last war. In eighteenth-century Germany, peasants apparently went to the lengths of starting forest fires to encourage them.

The morel's honeycomb structure means that it is apt to collect dirt and insects, and the caps must be cut in half and rinsed under running water before use. It is also usual to blanch them by dropping into boiling water for a few seconds.

Morels make good additions to stews and soups, and, being hollow, can be stuffed and baked. Carter's eighteenth-century *Herbal* gives a recipe for 'Fricassy of Morelles' – unusual for a time when fungi were generally regarded with suspicion:

'Cleanse them from the Sand by washing them, and brown a Piece of Butter gold colour, and toss them up, and their own Liquor will stove them; season them only with Pepper, Salt, and Nutmeg, and an Onion, and a little minc'd Parsley; when stov'd tender, toss them up as a Fricassy, with the Yolk of an Egg and a little White Wine, and a little Cream and thick Butter, and so serve them; and you may garnish with Lemon.'

Gymomitra esculenta   POISONOUS

The only species that might conceivably be mistaken for morels. Rather scarce, found under pines on sandy soils, and near the sites of bonfires in spring, like morel, but only really common in the central Highlands. Cap 2 to 4 inches (5 to 10 cm), with brain-like lobes, russet to rusty brown in colour. Flesh: pale, bitter, strong-smelling. Stem: short, stout, hollow.

HIGHLY POISONOUS when raw, but the toxins are destroyed by cooking.

The following morels are all edible and good:

Morchella rotunda

In woods on heavy soils. Late spring. Cap 4 to 8 inches (10 to 20 cm), yellowish brown. Stipe rather stocky.

Morchella vulgaris

As *M. esculenta* but with more sinuous and complex pitting.

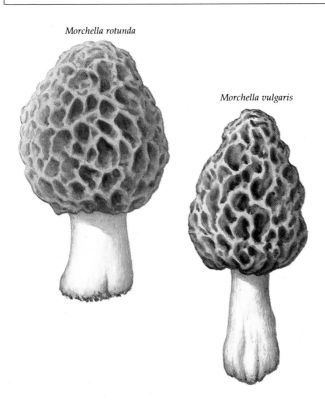

Morchella rotunda

Morchella vulgaris

Mitrophora semilibera

Quite common in damp copses on heavy soil in spring. Cap ¾ to 1½ inches (2 to 4 cm), olive-brown, slightly pitted with rather regular vertical ribs. Stipe creamy white, hollow.

TRUFFLE
Tuber aestivum

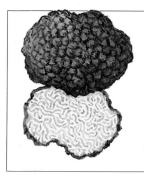

Truffles are a kind of underground fungus or mushroom, mostly about the size of a golf ball, blue-black in colour when fresh, turning to brown-black. The outside has a some-what warty appearance and inside the flesh is yellow-white with an average weight of a few ounces.

Truffles are all but impossible to find without specially trained animals. But there was once a lively traffic in them in some of the southern counties of England, where they were sniffed out of beech woods by Spanish poodles. It was a fascinating business, as this account shows, and worth reviving, for there is no reason why the truffles themselves should be any less plentiful.

'With the retirement in 1930 of Alfred Collins, the last of the professional truffle hunters, the English truffle industry ceased to exist, having been carried out in the Winterslow area of Wiltshire traditionally for 300 years. In themselves truffles do not have a great amount of taste but they have the virtue of spicing and bringing out the flavour of the ingredient they are cooked with, making them a highly-prized delicacy.

'In England they were found almost exclusively around the roots of beeches growing about three inches underground. The season lasted from November till March and Alfred Collins hunted for them far and wide with two trained dogs. . . . If hunting within about twenty miles of his home, Alfred Collins cycled, carrying one dog in a special leather bag while the other ran, changing them over every five miles. Both were carried home, however, after a tiring day's work. . . . The dogs have to be carefully looked after to avoid spoiling their noses; young ones are trained by tying them to an older one with a coupling strap. In its early days, the dog had a truffle rubbed on its nose to give it the scent. The dogs would dig up the truffles, usually being helped in the digging with a special small pronged fork so they would not become tired with their long exertions. On finding a truffle, the dog would pick it up in its mouth and the hunter had to remove it fairly quickly or the dog would eat it. Dogs were rewarded with pieces of bread.

'Pigs do not seem to have been much used in this country, which seems a little strange, as they hunt for truffles naturally, whereas dogs have to be trained. Normally, the hunter worked up wind and his dogs could scent the truffles frequently from a distance of twenty yards upwards. Truffles were invariably sold to private customers so they rarely came on the market. They only kept for about four days before losing flavour so they were always posted off as soon as possible in cardboard shoe boxes, which the children collected from the bootmaker for a penny each. Any not despatched were eaten by children on bread and butter. They could be preserved in vinegar. Like mushrooms they grew and then dispersed fairly quickly, the process taking about two days. If they grew more than six inches below the ground they were not much good.

'Alfred Collins could smell truffles and feel them underfoot and sometimes located them by the presence of a small cloud of flies in their vicinity. Some days, he drew completely blank, but on his best days he collected as many as 25 lbs. In about 1920, he put the price up to 2s 6d per pound, and by the time he retired he was able to get 5s 6d per pound. Even so, he died a poor man. His father once found a truffle weighing over 2 lb, which he sent to Queen Victoria, who replied saying she would send him her portrait. In due course, a sovereign arrived with her effigy on it.'

Condensed from 'Truffle Hunting in England' by J. E. Manners, *Country Life*, 7 January 1971

SPARASSIS
Sparassis crispa

Not uncommon at the base of pine stumps or trees, August
to November. Resembles a large round sponge, or the
heart of a cauliflower. The colour varies with age, from pale
cream to ochre. Size: about a foot (30 cm) across with *flat*,
twisted and very divided branches.

The only slightly dangerous species with which *Sparassis* could conceivably be confused is *Ramaria formosa*, which is rare, and has pink,
rounded branches.

If you are lucky enough to find a *Sparassis* nestling at the bottom
of a pine (the Swiss call it 'the Broody Hen') it should be cut off from
its thick fleshy stalk with a knife. Only young specimens should be
gathered as the old ones are tough and bitter.

Cut the *Sparassis* into sections and remove any brown or spongy
parts. Then wash thoroughly to remove any dirt and insects from
the folds. An old recipe for very young specimens is to bake them in
a casserole with butter, parsley, a little garlic, and some stock and
seasoning. They taste mild and pleasantly nutty.

Rather older specimens are best dried until they are brittle, for
future use as flavouring.

Ramaria formosa   **POISONOUS**

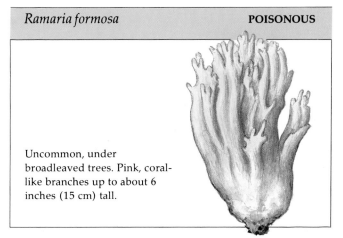

Uncommon, under broadleaved trees. Pink, coral-like branches up to about 6 inches (15 cm) tall.

Purgative, but not seriously poisonous.

HORN OF PLENTY
Craterellus cornucopoides

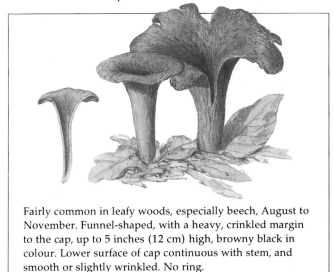

Fairly common in leafy woods, especially beech, August to November. Funnel-shaped, with a heavy, crinkled margin to the cap, up to 5 inches (12 cm) high, browny black in colour. Lower surface of cap continuous with stem, and smooth or slightly wrinkled. No ring.

Good for drying.

CHANTERELLE
Cantharellus cibarius

Fairly common in all kinds of woodland, but especially
beech, between July and December. Shaped like a funnel,
1 to 3 inches (2½ to 7½ cm) across. Egg-yolk yellow in
colour and smelling slightly of apricots. Gills like
fan-vaulting or veins, shallow, much forked and continuous
with the stem. No ring.

'You find them, suddenly, in the autumn woods, sometimes clus-
tered so close that they look like a torn golden shawl dropped
amongst the dead leaves and sticks.'

So Dorothy Hartley described this most exquisite of fungi. An
eighteenth-century writer said that if they were placed in the
mouths of dead men they would come to life again.

Because they are seldom attacked by insects, and cannot be confused with any dangerous species, chanterelles ('girolles') are perhaps the most used of all wild fungi on the Continent. They are
slightly tougher than some other fungi and should be stewed slowly
in milk for at least ten minutes. The result is delicately perfumed
and slightly peppery.

Perhaps because of colour sympathy chanterelles have always been associated with eggs, and there is scarcely any better way of serving previously cooked specimens than in omelettes or with scrambled eggs.

Two fairly common relations of *Chanterelle* are *Craterellus cornucopiodes* and *Cantharellus infundibuliformis*, both used in much the same way.

Cantharellus infundibuliformis

Fairly common in clusters in all kinds of woodland, July to January. Funnel-shaped, with a slightly crinkled margin. Cap: 1 to 2 inches (2½ to 5 cm) across and dark brown. Stem deep yellow. Gills: fold-like and branched as in the chanterelle. No ring.

WOOD HEDGEHOG
Hydnum repandum

Common in all kinds of woodland, August to November. The cap is irregularly shaped, about 2 to 4 inches (5 to 10 cm) across and is covered with a buffish to pink skin, smooth and often cracked, like fine leather. The 'gills' take

the form of unmistakable tiny white spines, of unequal length. Stem: short, stout, whitish. No ring.

The genus *Hydnum* is unique amongst fungi in having spines instead of gills, and all the commoner species having this characteristic are edible.

The wood hedgehog is the commonest species and is good to eat once its slightly bitter taste has been removed. This is best done by boiling the chopped fungus for a few minutes and then draining off and discarding the water. Then simmer in milk or stock for a further fifteen minutes. Serve on toast with a dash of sherry sprinkled over the top.

Sarcodon imbricatum

A close relative of the wood hedgehog. It is a conventionally shaped cap fungus, greyish brown in colour, with a scaly cap and the usual spiny gill structure of the *Hydnum* family. It occurs occasionally in sandy conifer woods between August and November, particularly in hilly districts.

It has an excellently strong, spicy flavour, and is consequently useful as a flavouring.

BEEFSTEAK FUNGUS
Fistulina hepatica

This is an aptly named bracket fungus, for the flesh when cut looks and feels like prime raw beef. It occurs occasionally on living trees, especially oak, and on the outside, to continue with meaty analogies, resembles an ox tongue. The top is reddish brown, and the underside covered with minute yellow pores.

Beefsteak Fungus

Regrettably, the beefsteak fungus does not really fulfil its visual promise, and the meat is rather tough and bitter. It is best chopped small and fried well with some other fairly strongly flavoured ingredients, such as onions and herbs. Even then the acrid taste is not completely destroyed, though in good specimens it is not unpleasantly reminiscent of unripe tomatoes.

ST GEORGE'S MUSHROOM
Tricholoma gambosum

Frequent on old grassland, downs and dunes throughout Britain, April to June. Cap 4 to 6 inches (10 to 15 cm), rounded, white to cream in colour. Gills, stipe and flesh white. Has a strong mealy, almost yeasty, smell.

This is the French *mousseron*, unmistakable as the only large white mushroom to appear in spring – traditionally around St George's Day, 23 April.

It is an excellent edible fungus, especially when gathered young. But some people find the aroma of mature specimens a little too heady and rich, and they are probably best used in dishes where there is another strongly flavoured ingredient – for instance in quiches with cheese and spinach or spring greens.

FIELD BLEWIT
Lepista saeva

Not uncommon in grassy pastures, October to December. The cap is flattish with an incurving marginal edge, 2 to 5 inches (5 to 12 cm) across, dry to touch but slightly jellyish and translucent, pale brown to greyish in colour. Gills: crowded, white to greyish-pink. Stem: stout, tinged with blue and occasionally swollen at the base. No ring. Flesh white and firm.

Blewits (named after the bluish-violet tinge of their stems) were one of the few fungi sold commercially in Britain. The trade was especially strong in the Midlands, and it is from there that the traditional way of cooking blewits as tripe comes.

Blewits often grow in large rings, and it is easy to overlook them in the late autumn, for their flat irregular caps look like dead leaves scattered over the field. Pick them on a dry day (they are very porous), clean, and chop off their stems. Then cut up the stems finely with an equal amount of onions and pack round the caps with a little chopped sage and bacon fat. Just cover the blewits with milk and simmer for half an hour. Pour off the liquid, thicken with flour and butter and seasoning and pour back over the fungi mixture. Simmer for another quarter of an hour, and then serve the whole mixture inside a ring of mashed potatoes, with toast and apple sauce.

This way of cooking the fungi is probably not entirely fortuitous, for their aromatic taste and jellyish texture are indeed reminiscent of tripe.

Fried with onions, and perhaps chopped potato, they also make an excellent omelette filling.

WOOD BLEWIT
Lepista nuda

Common in mixed woodlands and gardens, September to December. Much like the blewit, but bluish or violet all over when young. Cap: 2 to 4 inches (5 to 10 cm) across, turning reddish with age. Gills crowded, stem stout and mealy and always a little swollen at the base. No ring. Flesh tinged with violet at first, becoming whiter with age. Sweet smelling.

Use as field blewits, but do not eat raw, as they can be indigestible.

HONEY FUNGUS
Armillariella mellea

Abundant throughout Britain on tree stumps, roots, buried branches. A destructive parasite on all kinds of timber, recognisable from the black rhizomes encircling its host, which resemble a network of leather bootlaces. Caps 1½ to 3 inches (4 to 8 cm), in tufts, brownish scales on a honey yellow base. Gills creamy-white. Stipe yellowish, with a shaggy yellow ring.

Honey fungus caps can be fried when young, but they are rather rich, and experimenters should try a small quantity on the first testing. Probably best in stews.

ANISE CAP
Clitocybe odora

A small fungus which occurs in the litter of mixed woodlands in late summer and autumn. The whole fungus is a uniform blue-green colour, and has a strong, unmistakable smell of aniseed.

The aniseed smell persists on drying, and either fresh or dried the anise cap is used as a flavouring.

VELVET SHANK
Flammulina velutipes

Common in clusters on stumps and trunks between September and March. The caps are thin, about 1 to 3 inches (up to 7½ cm) across, sticky and glistening, and honey yellow to orange red in colour. Gills broad and pale yellow. Stem thin, tough, often curved. Dark brown in colour and covered with a dark velvety down. The flesh is thin, whitish and rubbery with no smell.

Velvet Shank

This is one of the few fungi able to survive through frosts. During the winter months there is consequently very little chance that it might be confused with another species.

They can even be picked while frozen, and either stored in a deep-freeze or added to stews and casseroles. Add a few towards the last stages of cooking a stew and they will float on the surface like fungal water-lilies.

FAIRY-RING CHAMPIGNON
Marasmius oreades

Very common on lawns and short grassland, April to December, often growing in 'fairy rings'. Cap 1⅛ to 2¾ inches (3 to 7 cm). The cap has a slight bump in the centre. When moist, the top is smooth and buffish in colour, and when dry, the skin wrinkles, becomes hard and leathery and changes to pale tan in colour. Gills, wide and usually free of the stipe, which is tough and fibrous. The smell is pleasantly aromatic, a little like new-mown hay scented with bitter almonds.

Fairy-ring Champignon

One of the best and most versatile toadstools – though care must be taken to distinguish it from somewhat similar small, white and poisonous *Clitocybe* species that can grow on lawns.

The fairy-ring champignon's natural tendency to dry out is one of its great virtues, and means that the caps can be easily preserved by threading them on to strings and hanging for a week or two in a dry, well-ventilated room. They can be reconstituted by soaking in water overnight.

Their other virtues are their almond fragrance and nutty texture. Add them to stews and casseroles – or fry them with chopped almonds or hazelnuts.

OYSTER MUSHROOM
Pleurotus ostreatus

Common round the year, though principally in autumn, on dead or dying branches of beech and ash. This is a bracket fungus, growing on the branch or trunk in shelves up to six inches (15 cm) across. The cap is shell-shaped, convex at

first, then flat, grey or slate-blue in colour. Gills white and deep. Flesh: white, soft, rubbery.

The oyster mushroom tends to be rather tough, and you should choose young specimens and cook them thoroughly. But when you find it, it is usually possible to gather considerable quantities from the clusters in which it invariably grows, so it should not be passed over. Try slicing into pieces not more than half an inch thick, sprinkling with a few drops of lemon juice, turning in seasoned flour, then in beaten egg and finally in breadcrumbs. The slices should then be fried in deep oil until golden. They can also be grilled, added to stew and casseroles, and dried.

Because of their comparatively mild flavour, oyster mushrooms can be served with fairly rich sauces. Try slicing them about 10 mm thick, and frying in oil for 5 minutes until their juices begin to flow. Sprinkle a little flour into the pan, and then stir in a glass of Madeira or sherry. Add a beaten egg yolk and seasoning. Then simmer and stir until the mixture thickens. Serve on toast or fried bread.

Oyster mushrooms are one of the few wild species that are now being successfully cultivated. Many supermarkets stock them, and it is possible to grow your own from specially prepared and pre-spawned 'logs'.

The *Amanita* family contains some of the commonest and most toxic of all poisonous fungi. All the dangerous species have a white sheath surrounding the base of the stem, a white ring, and white gills. Avoid *all* fungi that have this combination.

PANTHER CAP   POISONOUS
Amanita pantherina

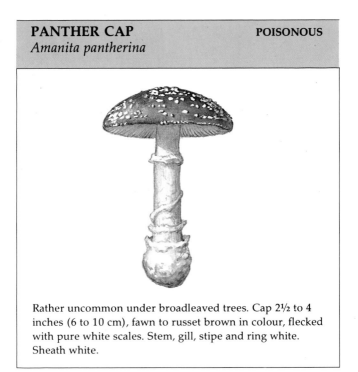

Rather uncommon under broadleaved trees. Cap 2½ to 4 inches (6 to 10 cm), fawn to russet brown in colour, flecked with pure white scales. Stem, gill, stipe and ring white. Sheath white.

DESTROYING ANGEL
Amanita virosa
POISONOUS

Uncommon, under broadleaved trees on acid soils. Cap 2 to 3 inches (5 to 8 cm). All parts – cap, gills, ring, stipe, sheath – pure white. DEADLY POISONOUS.

DEATH CAP
Amanita phalloides

POISONOUS

Quite common under broadleaf trees, and occasionally conifers. Cap 2½ to 5 inches (6 to 12 cm), smooth, yellowish green. Gill, stipe and ring white. Sheath very pronounced, like an open sack. DEADLY POISONOUS.

FLY AGARIC
Amanita muscaria

POISONOUS

Very common in birch and pine woods. Cap 4 to 8 inches (10 to 20 cm), bright vermilion, fading to orange, and usually flecked with white scales. Gills and stipe white. Ring white, with remnants of veil. Sheath white.

Fly Agaric

PARASOL MUSHROOM
Lepiota procera

Quite common in wood margins,
grassy clearings, roadsides, July to
November. A large fungus, up to 7
inches (18 cm) across. When young
the cap resembles an old-fashioned,
domed beehive. It then spreads out
flat but always retains its central
prominence. It is dry, scaly, brown
to grey-brown. Gills: white and
detached from the stem. Stem: tall,
slender, hollow and bulbous at the
base and slightly scaly like the cap.
Large white double ring which
eventually becomes completely free
of the stem so that it can be moved
up and down.

The parasol is one of the best of our edible fungi. It is also one of the most distinctive, and can often be seen from afar because of its size and preference for open spaces. The parasol rises closed, held to the stem by its large white ring. It then breaks free and opens like an umbrella. For the best combination of size and tenderness it should be picked just when the cap begins to open.

To cook, remove the stems and fry the caps quickly in oil or butter like field mushrooms. Because of their shape young parasols are also ideal for stuffing. Choose specimens that are still cup-shaped, cut off and discard the stems and fill with a sage and onion stuffing (or with mince or sausage meat if you want a more substantial dish). Arrange them their natural way up in a baking dish and fasten a small strip of bacon fat to the top of each parasol with a skewer. Cook in the oven for about half an hour, basting once or twice.

The shape of the more mature caps makes them suitable for making into fritters. Prepare the caps by removing the stalks, and wiping clean. Then dip them, whole, into flour, then batter, and deep fry in oil for about 5 minutes.

SHAGGY PARASOL
Lepiota rhacodes

Not uncommon on rich ground, though prefers more shade than the common parasol. July to November. Very similar to previous species, but cap is scalier and stem quite smooth. Flesh white but reddens on cutting.

Cook in the same way as common parasols.

FIELD MUSHROOM
Agaricus campestris

Locally common in pastures and meadows, August to November. Cap white, 1 to 3 inches (2½ to 7½ cm). Gills pink at first, darkening to brown. Stem short with a ring which in young specimens is joined to the cap. No sheath at base of stem, and no unpleasant smell.

Mushrooms have a special liking for meadows manured by horses, and the passing of horse-drawn transport has seriously affected the abundance of mushroom fields. There was a time when such fields might experience a 'white-out', when the precisely right combination of temperature, humidity and soil condition produced so many mushrooms simultaneously that the field appeared to have been covered overnight by snow. But in normal quantities they are, paradoxically, one of the less easy fungi to identify exactly. There is virtually nothing which could be mistaken for a sparassis or a chanterelle, but one or two white-capped meadow fungi which can be taken for mushrooms by the careless. But if you study cultivated mushrooms carefully, and go only for similar pink-gilled, sheathless specimens from the wild, you are unlikely to make a mistake.

Gathering mushrooms is a skill which has to be learned. They do not loom up above the grass like fairy story illustrations. In the rather dense pasture that is their natural habitat they are sometimes only visible as bright white patches in the grass when you are almost on top of them. You must train your eyes to scan no more then a few feet in front of you as you methodically quarter a field. When you find one, examine the area around it especially thoroughly, as mushrooms, like other fungi, tend to grow in colonies from the parent mycelium.

When you have your mushrooms check them again to make sure there are none with greenish-tinged or warty caps, or with remnants of sheath at the bottom of the stems. And until you are expert at recognising the 'jizz' of mushrooms it is as well to be doubly cautious and cut each specimen in half vertically. Discard any with pure white gills, or that quickly stain pink or yellow. The blusher (*Amanita rubescens*) and the yellow-staining mushroom (*Agaricus xanthodermus*) can both be mistaken for the field mushroom, and though neither of them is dangerously poisonous, they can cause digestive disturbances.

There is no need to peel mushrooms – indeed the taste will be diminished if you do. Simply wipe the caps with a dampish cloth and cut off the base of the stem. The very best way of cooking mushrooms is to fry them in bacon fat as soon as possible after collecting. The secret is to give them no more than three or four minutes in the pan. Field mushrooms tend to contain more water than cultivated, and if they are cooked for too long, they stew in their own liquid and become limp and mushy. Making soup from your wild mushrooms avoids this danger. Simply simmer the chopped caps and stems in seasoned milk for about half an hour with no other ingredients at all. Liquidise in a blender if desired. The result is a smooth, light soup which is good hot or cold.

Young field mushrooms can be used raw in salads, and ripe, dark-gilled ones for ketchup. Many other recipes came to light during the famous mushroom glut of autumn 1976. One of the more unusual is for mushroom pâté. Take about half a pound (225 gm) of mushrooms, chop up with one onion, a tomato and a rasher of bacon, and simmer slowly in a little oil until the mushrooms begin to sweat. If they give off a great deal of liquid, drain some of this away.

After simmering for ten minutes, cool and transfer to a blender and stir until the mixture is smooth. Return to the pan, add seasoning, herbs to taste and perhaps a pinch of chilli powder, and finally one beaten egg. Stir over a low heat until the texture thickens. Refrigerate for at least twelve hours, when it will acquire the consistency of a pâté, and a surprisingly meaty taste.

The following relatives of the field mushroom can all be treated in similar ways, and are all edible and good:

Agaricus haemorrhoidarius, Agaricus langei

Common under broadleaf trees. Cap 4 to 6 inches (10 to 15 cm), covered with reddish brown scales. Flesh white, flushing blood-red.

Agaricus silvaticus

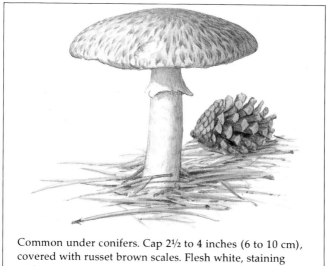

Common under conifers. Cap 2½ to 4 inches (6 to 10 cm), covered with russet brown scales. Flesh white, staining pink.

Agaricus silvicola

Common in woods, especially under beech and hornbeam. Cap 2½ to 5 inches (6 to 12 cm), white, turning yellow and eventually orange. Flesh white, then ochre. Smells of aniseed or gingerbread.

Agaricus macrosporus

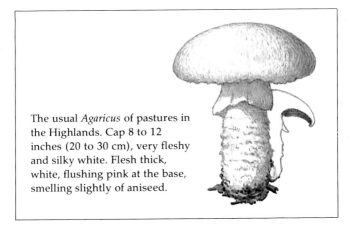

The usual *Agaricus* of pastures in the Highlands. Cap 8 to 12 inches (20 to 30 cm), very fleshy and silky white. Flesh thick, white, flushing pink at the base, smelling slightly of aniseed.

Agaricus augustus

Occasional in parks, gardens and broadleaf woods. Cap 5 to 7 inches (12 to 18 cm), covered with golden brown scales. Flesh white, flushing pink towards the base and yellowing in the cap. Smell of bitter almonds.

Agaricus bisporus

Fairly common in fields and gardens. Cap 2 to 4 inches (5 to 10 cm), white, browning slightly on the top. Flesh pinkening slightly with age.

This is the most common species in cultivation.

Agaricus bitorquis

Common in south-east England on waste ground, field edges, pavement cracks, etc. Cap 2½ to 5 inches (6 to 12 cm), white. Flesh dingy white, turning pale wine-coloured eventually. Smell almond-like.

HORSE MUSHROOM
Agaricus arvensis

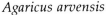

Very like a large field mushroom. Grows in similar habitats and at the same time of year. Can be up to 1 foot (30 cm) across when mature. Gills more greyish than in the field mushroom. Smells pleasantly of almonds.

This close cousin of the field mushroom is also becoming un-common. But it is a large, meaty and flavourful fungus, and if you only succeed in finding one mature specimen you have enough for a good meal.

If they are still dome-shaped they can be stuffed with whole toma-toes; if they are flat, grilled whole like steaks. An unusual recipe for either type is to stew them in milk, drain, set in a dish of white sauce, and then garnish with whole redcurrants made hot to the point of bursting. The dish is a contrast in colour and texture: the bright and sharp against the dark and fleshy.

Otherwise use as field mushroom.

YELLOW-STAINING MUSHROOM
Agaricus xanthodermus **POISONOUS**

Quite common in parks, open woodland, and gardens under broadleaf trees. Very similar in appearance to a small horse mushroom, except that the stipe turns bright chrome yellow if cut near the base. The smell is also distinctive, reminiscent of ink or iodine. Can cause acute, if temporary, digestive upsets in susceptible persons.

Agaricus placomyces   **POISONOUS**

Similar to the yellow stainer except that the cap is covered with dark scales. Indigestible rather than poisonous, but best avoided.

SHAGGY CAP
Coprinus comatus

Common in fields, road verges, playing fields, rubbish tips, June to November. Cap almost cylindrical at first, 2 to 5 inches (5 to 12 cm) high, white and covered with shaggy woolly scales. Opens to resemble a limp umbrella. Gills white at first, then pink to black as the cap opens, finally dissolving into an inky fluid. Stem, white and smooth with a small white ring at first.

The shaggy cap has a preference for grassland that is managed by humans rather than animals. It can often be found in large numbers in the short mown grass by roadsides, and even in the thin stripes between dual carriageways. It comes up like a white busby and can scarcely be mistaken for any other species, save perhaps its close relative *Coprinus atramentarius*. This too is edible, but can produce nausea if eaten together with alcohol. *Coprinus atramentarius* can be distinguished by its dirty grey colour, its absence of scales, its generally more slender build and lack of ring.

The shaggy cap should be gathered whilst the cap is still closed and the gills pale, and should be cooked as soon as possible after picking, before the cap starts to dissolve. Take off the stems and bake in a very slow casserole with cream or a mustard-flavoured roux for up to one hour. The taste is pleasant and mild, a little like shellfish in texture, but perhaps too innocuous to some palates.

You can capitalise on their deliquescent nature and turn them into ketchup. Put the young caps into an earthenware jar, pack them down well and strew each layer with salt. When the jar is full put it in the oven, and simmer for an hour or two, being careful not to lose too much liquid by evaporation. Then strain through muslin, and for each quart of liquid add an ounce of black pepper and a scrape of nutmeg. Boil up again, strain into clean (preferably sterilised)

Shaggy Cap

bottles and seal well. The ketchup will keep indefinitely, but should be used quickly once opened.

A nice conceit is to open a cap so that it resembles a starfish, remove the stem and place it on top of a raw egg in a dish. Then bake in a medium oven for a quarter of an hour.

RED-STAINING INOCYBE
Inocybe patouillardii

POISONOUS

Uncommon in woodland glades, parks, etc. Cap 2 to 2¾ inches (5 to 7 cm), conical. Gills, stipe and flesh whitish, but soon reddening with age or bruising. Smell fruity.

Many inocybe species are toxic, but most grow in woodland habitats, not in the open grassland favoured by the fairy-ring champignon. The most seriously poisonous member of the family, red-staining inocybe, is unfortunately sometimes an exception.

AVOID ALL INOCYBES.

Galerina mutabilis

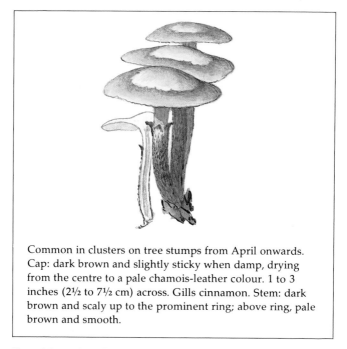

Common in clusters on tree stumps from April onwards. Cap: dark brown and slightly sticky when damp, drying from the centre to a pale chamois-leather colour. 1 to 3 inches (2½ to 7½ cm) across. Gills cinnamon. Stem: dark brown and scaly up to the prominent ring; above ring, pale brown and smooth.

One of the earliest fungi to appear, and difficult to confuse with any other species if it is picked in the spring.

Although the caps are rather small and thin-fleshed, the clusters can contain literally hundreds, and certainly enough for a good meal. The fungus has an agreeable flavour, and is excellent for flavouring soups and stews, to which it gives a rich brown colour.

CEP
Boletus edulis

Quite common in rides and clearings in all sorts of woods, especially beech, August to November. Cap, brown, dry and smooth, 2 to 6 inches (5 to 15 cm) across. Gills in

Cep

Boletus are replaced by pores, much like sponge rubber in appearance, and in *Boletus edulis*, yellow to olive-brown in colour. Stem short and bulging, pale brown streaked with white. No ring. Flesh white and firm, and pleasant smelling.

All members of the *Boletus* family are distinguishable by their 'gills', which are a spongy mass of fine tubes beneath the cap. The cep has the additional distinction of looking exactly like a glossy penny bun, to which it is always compared.

Ceps are one of the most famous of all edible fungi and at one time there were six different varieties for sale at Covent Garden. Unfortunately they are equally well liked by insects, so it is as well to cut the caps in half before cooking to check that they are not infested. To prepare for cooking remove the stem, and scoop away the pores with a spoon (unless they are very young and firm).

There are a prodigious number of recipes for ceps. They can be sliced and fried in oil for ten minutes with a little garlic and parsley. They can be fried with potatoes, or grilled with fish. They are excellent for drying (and indeed in the dried form are quite widely available in delicatessens in this country).

One of the most attractive is an old Polish recipe for beetroot and cep soup, which is served on Christmas Eve. Make some clear beetroot stock by boiling chopped raw beetroots in water, with bay leaves and peppercorns. Take your sliced ceps and fry in butter with chopped onion and paprika pepper for about five minutes. Take some ravioli-shaped pasta cases and fill with the cep and onion mixture, minced fine. Seal the cases, and bake in the oven until golden-brown. Reheat the beetroot stock, and sharpen to taste with a little vinegar and lemon juice. At the last minute add the hot cases and serve.

Most *Boletus* species are mild and nutty to taste, and they are amongst the most popular edible fungi on the Continent.

There are a large number of boletes growing in the British Isles, and all of them have the same foam-like gill structure. A few are indigestible or can cause bad gastric upsets. Luckily all of these are coloured red or purple on pores or stem, and so are easily avoidable. None of the *edible* species described below has this feature.

Boletus subtomentosus

Quite common in all sorts of wood, especially in moss and on grassy paths, June to October. Cap 2 to 3 inches (5 to 7½ cm) across, colour varied, olive-yellow to brown; when old the surface is often cracked. Pores bright yellow. Stem yellow-brown, ribbed, tapering towards the base. Flesh soft, yellowish-white, pleasant smelling.

Boletus badius (also known as *Xerocomus badius*)

Quite common under conifers, August to November. Very similar to *Boletus edulis*. Cap 2 to 4 inches (5 to 10 cm) across, chestnut to chocolate brown, felt-like when dry, but

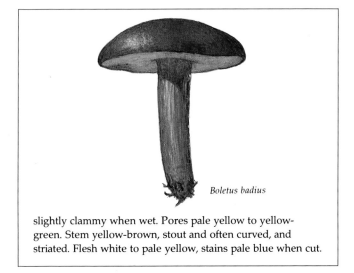

Boletus badius

slightly clammy when wet. Pores pale yellow to yellow-green. Stem yellow-brown, stout and often curved, and striated. Flesh white to pale yellow, stains pale blue when cut.

Boletus cyanescens (also known as *Gyroporus cyanescens*)

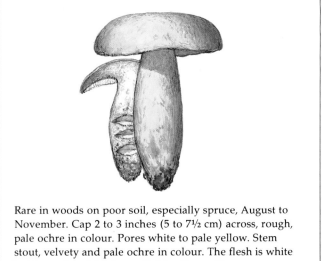

Rare in woods on poor soil, especially spruce, August to November. Cap 2 to 3 inches (5 to 7½ cm) across, rough, pale ochre in colour. Pores white to pale yellow. Stem stout, velvety and pale ochre in colour. The flesh is white but turns deep blue immediately after cutting.

Boletus luteus (also known as *Suillus luteus*)

Quite common amongst grass in conifer woods, September to November. Cap 2 to 3 inches (5 to 7½ cm) across, orange-brown, tinged with purple, and slimy to the touch. Pores white to pale yellow. Stem yellow, with a brownish-purple ring. Flesh yellow, unchanging when cut.

Peel before cooking. Will not keep and therefore unsuitable for drying.

Boletus granulatus (also known as *Suillus granulatus*)

Quite common in conifer woods, June to October. Cap 2 to 3 inches (5 to 7½ cm) across, slimy, straw-yellow to leather-brown. Peels easily. Pores yellow to olive, and when young exudes milky drops. Stem slender, light yellow. Flesh yellowish, unchanging when cut, fruity to smell. (Very susceptible to maggots.)

Boletus luteus

Boletus granulatus

Boletus flavus (also known as *Suillus grevillii*)

Quite common in larch woods only, March to November. Cap 2 to 4 inches (5 to 10 cm), slimy, pale yellow. Pores sulphur yellow. Stem tall, yellowish brown, with a distinctive yellow ring. Flesh has the colour and texture of rhubarb and stains pale lilac on cutting.

Boletus satanas   POISONOUS

Locally common under broadleaf trees in the south. Cap large, 6 to 12 inches (15 to 30 cm), almost hemispherical and entirely white, turning greyish with age. Pores red. Stipe rounded and covered with red veining. Smell very unpleasant.

Very indigestible, and causing acute gastric attacks in some eaters.

Boletus erythropus

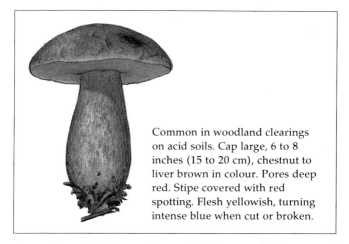

Common in woodland clearings on acid soils. Cap large, 6 to 8 inches (15 to 20 cm), chestnut to liver brown in colour. Pores deep red. Stipe covered with red spotting. Flesh yellowish, turning intense blue when cut or broken.

An excellent edible fungus, but probably best avoided because of the possibility of misidentification of *B. satanas*. Similarly take care with *B. luridus*, *B. quelitii* and *B. rhodopurpureus*.

Leccinum scabrum

Common in grass under birches, July to November. Cap 2 to 4 inches (5 to 10 cm) across, smooth and greyish-brown, dry, but sticky in wet weather. Gills white to dirty fawn. Stem tall, white, flecked with brown to black scales. Flesh soft, soon becoming moist and spongy. (Usually fairly free of maggots.)

Leccinum versipelle

Common under birches and conifers, July to November.
Cap 3 to 7 inches (8 to 18 cm) across, orange-yellow to
yellow-brown. Pores minute, dirty grey. Stem sturdy and
tapering towards the cap, slate coloured, scurfy. Flesh
white, very slowly turning dirty pink on cutting. (Don't be
alarmed by the fact that the flesh turns black on cooking.)

THE *RUSSULA* SPECIES

The *Russulas* are a difficult family, multi-specied, enormously vari-
able in colouring and yet too good to omit altogether. Their variabil-
ity can lead almost any specimen, at some stage in its development,
to become one of those vague white-gilled, yellowish, greenish or
brownish capped fungi which are so difficult to tell from the main
poisonous species. In fact, none of the *Russulas* themselves are poisonous when cooked.

Russula vesca

Russula vesca is probably the easiest of the common species to identify. It grows in all sorts of woods, especially oak and beech, from June to November. The cap is 2 to 4 inches (5 to 10 cm) across, and can be coloured anything from pale pink to violet or rusty red. Stem and gills are pure white, and there is no ring or sheath. The best identifying feature is the fact that, when the fungus is mature, one or two millimetres of the margin of the cap are free from skin, and finely grooved with radial veins.

Cooked like a *Boletus*, *Russula vesca* is an excellent fungus, firmer than most, and with a mildly nutty taste which has been likened to new potatoes.

Russula claroflava

Common under birch.
Cap 3⅛ to 4½ inches (8 to 12 cm), yellow matt at first, then shiny. Gills ochre, stipe white, bruising greyish.

One of the best of the *Russulas*.

Russula virescens

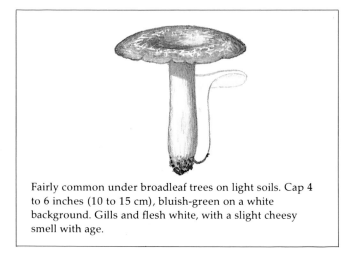

Fairly common under broadleaf trees on light soils. Cap 4 to 6 inches (10 to 15 cm), bluish-green on a white background. Gills and flesh white, with a slight cheesy smell with age.

Russula xerampelina

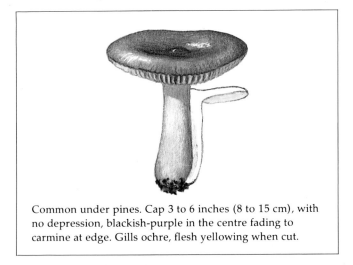

Common under pines. Cap 3 to 6 inches (8 to 15 cm), with no depression, blackish-purple in the centre fading to carmine at edge. Gills ochre, flesh yellowing when cut.

Russula atropurpurea

Common throughout Britain, especially under oak. Cap 3⅛ to 5⅞ inches (8 to 15 cm), a striking deep purple in colour, with a darker centre. Gills, stipe and flesh dull white, smelling slightly of apples.

THE SICKENER   POISONOUS
Russula emetica

Common under conifers. Another variety grows under beeches. Cap 1⅛ to 4 inches (3 to 10 cm), bright cherry red or vermilion. Gills and flesh white, with a distinctive smell of coconut.

POISONOUS WHEN RAW AND BEST AVOIDED ALTOGETHER.

Russula aeruginea

Quite common under birch and conifers. Cap 3⅛ to 4⅝ inches (8 to 12 cm), with no central depression. Greenish-grey in colour. Gills forked and bright yellow. Stipe white, yellowing slightly with age.

Russula cyanoxantha

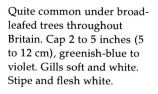

Quite common under broad-leafed trees throughout Britain. Cap 2 to 5 inches (5 to 12 cm), greenish-blue to violet. Gills soft and white. Stipe and flesh white.

Russula rosea

Common under broadleaf trees, especially beech. Cap 3⅛ to 4⅝ inches (8 to 12 cm), slightly depressed in the centre. Cap a delicate pink fading towards the centre. Gills and flesh white, with no distinctive smell or taste.

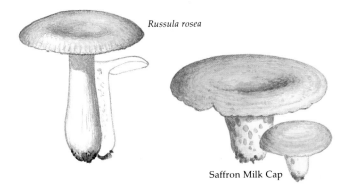

Russula rosea

Saffron Milk Cap

SAFFRON MILK CAP
Lactarius deliciosus

Widespread in pine woods, provided the soil is not too acid. Cap 4 to 8 inches (10 to 20 cm), orange-red, with darker banding, and orange-yellow gills.

The whole fungus exudes beads of orange milk, sometimes slightly bitter in taste. A popular fungus in parts of Europe, but too rich (and occasionally bitter) for some tastes.

Calvatia utriformis

Common throughout Britain on lawns, pastures and sand-dunes. About 1⅛ to 2⅜ inches (3 to 6 cm) across, with no stipe. Entirely white or cream in colour, with a slightly mealy surface.

GIANT PUFFBALL
Langermannia gigantea

Not uncommon in woods, fields and under hedges. August
to October. A large spherical fungus, 4 to 12 inches (10 to
30 cm) across, white, smooth and leathery initially, turning
yellow to green when old. Grows apparently straight from
the ground, with little or no stalk. Flesh solid, spongy, and
pure white when young.

I think that if I had to choose my own favourite species from this
book it would be the giant puffball. To come upon one of these suddenly is a memorable experience, only rivalled by the taste of the
first mouthful. There is not much point in searching deliberately for
them; they are always unexpected, glinting like huge displaced eggs
under a hedge or in the corner of a field. It always seems sad to
butcher the soft, kid-leather skin; but when you do cut through the
flesh, the great flaky slabs of white meat that fall away are just as
inviting.

Giant puffballs can grow to a prodigious size. Some have been
found four feet (over 1 m) in diameter. The usual size is more like a
small football, but even this will provide a feast for a large number of
people, for every part of the fungus is solid, edible flesh.

The only important quality to look out for is that this flesh is still
pure white. As they age puffballs turn yellowish brown, and finally
dissolve into a dust which consists of the reproductive spores. The
giant puffball is one of the most fecund of all living organisms, and a
single specimen may produce up to seven billion spores. If all of

these germinated successfully and produced similar specimens with equally successful spores, their grandchildren would form a mass eight hundred times the volume of the earth.

There is no real need to peel puffballs, though the skin may be too leathery for some tastes. One simple but excellent way to cook them is to slice them into large steaks about half an inch thick. Fry these, straight or battered, in bacon fat for about ten minutes until they are golden brown. The slices taken from the smoother, more rubbery flesh near the top of the fungus are like sweetbreads; the more crumbly steaks from near the base are as succulent as toasted marshmallow.

Even with small specimens you are likely to be left with some perfectly good surplus flesh, and some collectors have experimented with deep-freezing this; the slices may either be used fresh or coated in egg and breadcrumbs and pre-cooked. But the results, though perfectly edible, tend to be too soggy to be worth repeating. Perhaps the answer is not to pick the whole puffball at once, as recommended in a Victorian book: 'We have known specimens to grow amongst cabbages in a kitchen garden, and when such is the case it may be left standing, slices being cut off as required until the whole is consumed.'

A more radical solution is to cook the whole ball at once, stuffed. You need to hollow it out until there is a shell about 1 inch (2.5 cm) thick remaining. Fill it with a mixture of mince, herbs, rice and the crumbled-up hollowings. Wrap with bacon and metal foil and bake in a medium oven for about one hour. The very heavy aroma during cooking may put off some people, but at least the ball resembles a roast turkey when it emerges from the oven.

There are a number of different species of puffball growing in this country, all resembling more or less miniature versions of the giant puffball. All are edible when young and white-fleshed. But there is a species of a related family, the common earth-ball, which can cause gastric upsets if eaten in quantity. This resembles a puffball in shape, but its surface is hard, brown and scaly. So it is as well to pick only those puffballs which are white or creamy, and relatively smooth skinned.

It is usual to peel these smaller balls, as the skin can be tougher than the giant puffball's. This, together with the cutting of the base, will tell you if the flesh is white inside. These smaller balls can be cooked like *Langermannia gigantea*, or stewed whole in milk.

The commonest species is the common puffball:

COMMON PUFFBALL
Lycoperdon perlatum

Very common in pastures, heaths and sometimes woods, from June to November. 1 to 3 inches (2½ to 7½ cm) across. More pear-shaped than spherical, skin white to cream when young, usually covered with tiny, spiny pimples.

JEW'S EAR
Auricularia auricula-judae

Quite common on elder trees throughout the year, especially October and November. An ear-shaped bracket fungus, 1 to 3 inches (2½ to 7½ cm) across, usually growing in clusters. Red-brown in colour, and gelatinous and soft when young. Upper surface more velvety and brown, underside more pink.

I can imagine no food more forbidding in appearance than the Jew's ear. It hangs in folds from decaying elder branches like slices off some ageing kidney, clammy and jelly-like to the touch. It is no fungus to leave around the house if you have sensitive relations, or even to forget about in your own pocket.

But it is a good edible species for all that, and is much prized in China, where a related species is grown for food on oak palings. It was also valued by the old herbalists (as 'fungus sambuci') as a poultice for inflamed eyes, though apparently not sufficiently to warrant a more complimentary name; 'Jew's meat' was the deprecatory term for all fungi in the Middle Ages. (Though the name may contain an oblique reference to Judas, who reputedly hanged himself from an elder tree.)

Jew's ear should be gathered whilst it is still soft (it turns rock-hard with age) and cut from the tree with a knife. It should be washed well, and sliced finely, for although the translucent flesh is thin, it can be tough and indigestible. Stew for a good three-quarters of an hour in stock or milk, and serve with plenty of pepper. The result is crisp and not unlike a seaweed.

An unusual sweet soup is made with the very similar 'cloud ears' in China. Clean and soak 1 oz (28 gm) of Jew's ears and chop roughly. Heat 2 lb (900 gm) of brown sugar crystals in 1 pt (568 ml) of water until the sugar melts and the mixture is almost boiling. Drain the ears, add to the syrup and steam for 1½ hours. Serve hot or cold.

SHELLFISH

It is believed that many of the more bloodcurdling superstitions associated with the Mandrake – in particular its power to flee from prospective pickers on leg-like roots, or kill them off with its notorious shriek – were invented by professional Greek herb pickers, who were anxious to keep amateurs away from their livelihood. The same is probably true of many of the stories concerning the poisonousness of shellfish out of season. Shellfish are one of the lifelines by which coastal dwellers hang on to a measure of independence round the year. Yet they are also one of the most tempting of wild foods that are there just for the picking. Unhappily for the professionals, the next generation of pickings is being spawned just when the holidaymakers are trooping out to the mudflats with their buckets and spades. No wonder, then, that the gentle warnings of superstition, the one sort of 'Keep Out' notice permissible on public land, are propped up rather more than they would be by facts alone.

In fact every sort of fish is slightly out of condition during the breeding season, but none need be poisonous, not even shellfish. This is not to say that there are no good reasons for leaving shellfish alone during the summer months. Molluscs are highly susceptible to disease and temperature change, and unless the largest possible numbers are allowed to spawn freely, their survival rate will be low.

And ironically, the way we are currently treating our coastal waters may yet turn the story into sound advice. Bivalve molluscs (with shells in two hinged halves like castanets) feed by pumping water through their shells and filtering out the food particles. In doing this they may also filter out sewage particles and the enteric bacteria which are associated with them. During the warm weather which corresponds to the off-season these bacteria can multiply alarmingly, up to a level which can cause food poisoning in humans. Unfortunately this is particularly true of large bivalves like mussels and oysters, which filter a great deal of water each day, and sometimes seem to relish the warm, soupy conditions near sewage outlets.

So shellfish should be approached with caution, but not with trepidation, and with the knowledge that it is not some sinister springtime sap that makes them chancy during the warm months, but our own disgusting habits.

RULES

If you keep to these few rules, you will never need a stomach pump:

1 Never gather them close to human dwellings, or anywhere where sewage or refuse is pumped into the sea.

2 Always wash them well, outside and in, in clean water.

3 Check that all your specimens are alive immediately before cooking them. Shellfish decompose very quickly after death, and a dead fish is more dangerous than a dirty one. To tell if a shellfish is alive, gently force its shell open a fraction of an inch. It should shut again quickly as soon as you take off the pressure. If it is already open, opens wide with ease, or fails to shut again, it is safer to assume that it is dead.

LIMPET
Patella vulgata

Limpets are shaped like flat cones and cling to rocks. The common limpet, *Patella vulgata*, is common enough on rocky shores, and can grow up to 2½ inches (6 cm) across. But it is normally somewhat smaller than this, and consequently a fair number – and a fair degree of scrambling – are needed to gather enough for a meal.

Do not pick them from piers or jetties, but from out-of-town rocks that are covered daily by the tide. They can be prised from the rocks with a knife. Soak them in the usual way and then boil like cockles until the meat floats free of the shell. Be warned, though: limpets can be very tough, and they may need considerable further simmering or baking. In the Isle of Man they fry them at Easter.

WINKLE
Littorina littorea

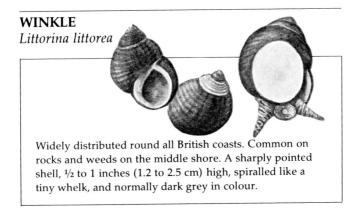

Widely distributed round all British coasts. Common on rocks and weeds on the middle shore. A sharply pointed shell, ½ to 1 inches (1.2 to 2.5 cm) high, spiralled like a tiny whelk, and normally dark grey in colour.

You will not need to spend very long unravelling a bowl of winkles from their tortuous shells before you appreciate why the process produced a new verb of extrication for the English language.

Judged purely as food, winkles do not have much to commend them. They have none of the rich flavour of mussels or the he-man texture of whelks. You need a dozen to provide a single mouthful. The joy of winkle eating lies wholly in the challenge of getting the things out of their shells, and, for the experienced, in the leisurely ritual of the pin and the twist. Dorothy Hartley describes a delightful encounter with a connoisseur:

'I learnt "winkles" from a night watchman. He used to sit by his big red coke fire-bucket, a bit of folded blanket over his knees, his mug of hot tea, and a little enamel bowl full of winkles. And he would turn up the little tab-end at the bottom of his waistcoat, pull out a long pin, and take a winkle. . . . And then he would chuck the empty shell neatly over his shoulder into the canal with a tiny "plop". He did it quite slowly, and he always paused (I can see him now, red in the fire-light, head aslant, his huge hand still half-open – curved like a hoary brown shell). He always paused just that second till he heard the tiny plop, before he bent and picked up the next winkle. His old woman had put him "a reet proper breakfast", and he had a basket with a bottle in it. But, as he said, "Winkles, they *do* pass the time along very pleasantly".

From *Food in England*.

You can find winkles on almost every stretch of rocky or weedy shore between high and low tide-marks. They are often in quite large colonies, and can be easily gathered.

To clean the sand and grit out from them thoroughly, soak them in fresh water for about twelve hours. Then cook them by plunging them into boiling water and simmering for about ten minutes.

Then eat them like the night watchman, leisurely, with a long pin, and perhaps a little salt and vinegar at the side. The whole fish is edible, except for the tiny mica-like plate at the mouth of the shell, which should be removed with your pin before you winkle out the flesh.

MUSSEL
Mytilus edulis

The edible mussel is up to 4 inches (10 cm) long and has a blue-black shell with a pearly, whitish lining.

Mussels are amongst our commonest and most delectable shellfish. But they are also responsible for most cases of shellfish poisoning.

If you follow the tips given on p. 221 you are unlikely to eat a bad mussel. Gather them from clean stony shores at low tide outside the summer months, let them stand through at least two changes of fresh tapwater, and check that each one is still alive before cooking.

If you only have a few, try baking them in their shells in hot ash, and popping in a mixture of butter garlic and parsley as the shells open.

SCALLOP
Pecten maximus

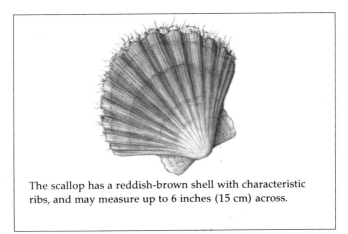

The scallop has a reddish-brown shell with characteristic ribs, and may measure up to 6 inches (15 cm) across.

This is the classic shell that came to be the oil company's symbol. You find them occasionally on the lower shore – that strip of sand that is only uncovered during very low tides.

Like clams, scallops need careful cooking. After washing and scalding, cut away the white and orange fish, dust with flour or breadcrumbs and fry for about ten minutes. They have a superbly fleshy, almost poultry-like flavour.

OYSTER
Ostrea edulis

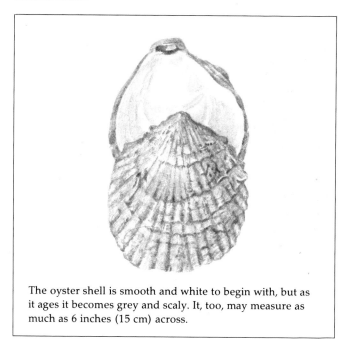

The oyster shell is smooth and white to begin with, but as it ages it becomes grey and scaly. It, too, may measure as much as 6 inches (15 cm) across.

Oysters have not always been the expensive delicacy that they are now. For centuries they were one of the great staples of working-class diet. In the latter half of the nineteenth century prices suddenly rocketed, and there is little doubt that the cause was the irresponsible over-harvesting of the beds to meet the demands of expanding townships.

Today you will be lucky to find many wild oysters. The ones that still remain round our coasts are mostly under cultivation in private beds. So if you should chance upon one, clinging to a rock in some estuary or creek, best leave it where it is. But if eat it you must, there is only one way: raw, with lemon and tabasco sauce.

COCKLE
Cardium edule

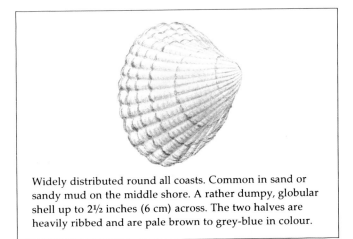

Widely distributed round all coasts. Common in sand or sandy mud on the middle shore. A rather dumpy, globular shell up to 2½ inches (6 cm) across. The two halves are heavily ribbed and are pale brown to grey-blue in colour.

Just after the tide has gone out over the vast saltmarshes on the north Norfolk coast, you will sometimes see a cluster of enormous slate-coloured cockles strewn across the muddy sand like dice. These are the famous 'Stiffkey Blues', the best and fattest cockles of all.

To find any cockles, big or small, as conspicuously displayed as this is a rare piece of luck. More often they are one to three inches under the surface. There is no simple rule about where they can be found between the tidelines. A vein of mud in the sand is a good sign; so is a green film of plankton over the surface. But the only sure test is to scratch about and see if they are there. Hands will do if you only want a few, but a rake with blunted points is the best way of pulling them out of the sand quickly. Gather them into a bucket or bag. Do not throw them; the shells break easily, and a broken cockle is very quickly a dead one. Don't pick any specimen less than one inch across either. It's scarcely worth the bother. And cockles, like all shellfish, wage a constant battle for survival against pollution and over-picking. If the young fish are taken before they have had a chance to spawn then the battle is bound to be a losing one. Many stretches of coast have experienced shellfish droughts recently, and though there is probably no single explanation, the over-picking of immature shells is certainly a contributing factor.

When you have all the cockles you want take them home and wash off the superficial mud and sand. Let them rinse themselves through in a bucket of clean, fresh water for at least six hours, and preferably overnight. Then drop them into a saucepan of boiling water, checking each one for signs of life immediately before. They will quickly open, and be thoroughly cooked within five minutes.

The results can be made into soups or pies, or eaten plain as soon as they have been strained from the water. Try experimenting with sauces to go with the freshly cooked fish. A friend of mine once concocted one out of the improbable ingredients of yoghourt, mustard and horseradish, and it made a wonderfully tart, silky foil to the springy flesh of the cockles. One eighteenth-century cookery book recommends that the cooked fish should be stuffed into slits in marsh lamb, as if the meat were larded with them.

My favourite way with cockles is to fry them with bacon. Cook the bacon very crisp first, then remove it from the pan and fry the cockles in its fat. Serve them together on toast with plenty of pepper.

CLAM, SAND GAPER
Mya arenaria

Widely distributed. Common in sand and sandy mud on the middle and lower shore. An oval shell not unlike a large mussel in shape, up to 5 inches (12½ cm) across, coloured grey or brownish.

Clams are big enough to need substantially more cooking than most shellfish. After the shells have been rinsed like cockles, they are scalded in boiling water for about ten minutes. The fish is then removed from the shell, the siphon usually trimmed off, and the remaining meat fried or baked for a further half an hour, or simply boiled until tender and served with a sauce.

SOURCES, REFERENCES AND FURTHER READING

GENERAL AND HISTORICAL

AUSTIN, THOMAS (ed.), *Two Fifteenth Century Cook Books*, Early English Text Society, 1888

BROTHWELL, DON and PATRICIA, *Food in Antiquity*, 1969

BURKILL, I. H., *Habits of Man, and the Origins of Cultivated Plants in the Old World*, Proc. Linn. Soc. 164, 1953

CANDOLLE, A. DE, *Origines des Plantes Cultivées*, Paris, 1883

CULPEPER, NICHOLAS, *The Complete Herbal*, 1653

DRUMMOND, C., and WILBRAHAM, ANNE, *The Englishman's Food*, 1957

EVELYN, JOHN, *Acetaria: A Discourse of Sallets*, 1699. Facsimile, 1982

GERARD, JOHN, *The Herbal*. Revised and enlarged by Thomas Johnson, 1633 (facsimile edition Dover, New York, 1975)

GILES, W. F., 'Our vegetables, whence they came', *Royal Horticultural Society Journal*, Vol. 69, 1944

GODWIN, H., *The History of the British Flora*, 1956

GREENOAK, FRANCESCA, *Forgotten Fruit*, 1983

GRIGSON, GEOFFREY, *The Englishman's Flora*, 1958. Revised ed., 1987

GRIGSON, GEOFFREY, *A Herbal of all sorts*, 1959

GRIGSON, JANE, *Jane Grigson's Fruit Book*, 1982

GRIGSON, JANE, *Jane Grigson's Vegetable Book*, 1978

HARTLEY, DOROTHY, *Food In England*, 1954

HELBAEK, H., 'Studying the diet of ancient man', *Archaeology* 14, 1961

HENSLOW, G., 'The origin and history of our garden vegetables', *Royal Horticultural Society Journal*, Vols. 36, 37, 1910–11

HUTCHINS, SHEILA, *English Recipes*, 1967

HYAMS, EDWARD, *Plants in the service of man*, 1971

JOHNSON, CHARLES, *The useful plants of Great Britain*, 1862

LOVELOCK, YANN, *The vegetable book*, 1972

MARKHAM, GERVASE, *The English Hus-Wife*, 1615

MASEFIELD, G. B., WALLIS, M., HARRISON, S. G., NICHOLSON, B. E., *The Oxford Book of Food Plants*, 1969

MEAD, W. E., *The English medieval feast*, 1931

MINISTRY OF AGRICULTURE, *British poisonous plants*, 1954. Revised edition, 1986

NORTH, PAMELA, *Poisonous plants and fungi*, 1967

PIRIE, N. W., *Food Resources: conventional and novel*, 1969

SALISBURY, SIR EDWARD, *Weeds and aliens*, 1961

SOLE, WILLIAM, *Menthae Britannicae*, 1798

STEARN, W. T., 'The origin and later development of cultivated plants', *Royal Horticultural Society Journal*, Vol. 90, 1965

STEVENSON, VIOLET (ED.), *A Modern Herbal*, 1974

TREASE, G. E., *A textbook of pharmacognosy*, 1961

TUDGE, COLIN, *Future Cook*, 1980

TURNER, WILLIAM, *The Herbal*, 1568

WALLIS, T. E., *Textbook of pharmacognosy*, 1960

WHITE, FLORENCE, *Good things in England*, 1968

WILSON, C. ANNE, *Food and drink in Britain*, 1973

WILD FOOD GUIDES
(British and European)

ELEY, GEOFFREY, *Wild Fruits and Nuts*, 1976

ELEY, GEOFFREY, *101 Wild plants for the kitchen*, 1977

HATFIELD, AUDREY WYNNE, *How to enjoy your weeds*, 1969

HEDRICK, U. P. (ed.), *Sturtevant's edible plants of the world* (1919), new ed. 1970

HILL, JASON, *The wild foods of Britain*, 1939

JORDAN, MICHAEL, *A guide to wild plants*, 1976

LOEWENFELD, CLAIRE, and BACK, PHILIPPA, *The complete book of herbs and spices*, 1974

LOEWENFELD, CLAIRE, *Nuts*, 1957

MAUDUIT, VICOMTE DE, *They can't ration these*, 1940

MICHAEL, PAMELA, *All good things around us*, 1980

MINISTRY OF FOOD, *Hedgerow Harvest*, 1943

PETERSON, VICKI, *The natural food catalogue*, 1978

PHILIPPS, ROGER, *Wild food*, 1983

RICHARDSON, ROSAMUND, *Hedgerow cookery*, 1980

RANSON, F., *British herbs*, 1949

SCOTT, AMORET, *Hedgerow harvest*, 1979

URQUHART, JUDY, *Living off nature*, 1980

WHITE, FLORENCE, *Flowers as food*, 1952

WILD FOOD GUIDES
(North American, but worth consulting as
there is a considerable overlap between species)

ANGIER, BRADFORD, *Wilderness cookery*, Stackpole Books, 1970

ASSINIWI, BERNARD, *Survival in the bush*, Copp Clark, 1972

BRACKETT, B., and LASH, M., *The wild gourmet*, David Godine, 1975

GIBBONS, EUELL, *Stalking the blue-eyed scallop*, David McKay, 1966

GIBBONS, EUELL, *Stalking the healthful herbs*, David McKay, 1966

GIBBONS, EUELL, *Stalking the wild asparagus*, David McKay, 1962

HARRINGTON, H. D., *Edible native plants of the Rocky Mountains*,
   University of New Mexico Press, 1967

HARRIS, BEN CHARLES, *Eat the weeds*, Barre, 1972

HITCHCOCK, SUSAN TYLER, and MCINTOSH, G. B., *Gather ye wild
   things*, Harper and Row, 1980

LAUREL, ALICIA BAY, *Living on the earth*, 1971

MEDSGER, OLIVER PERRY, *Edible wild plants*, Macmillan, New York,
   1966

WEINER, MICHAEL A., *Earth medicine – earth foods*, Collier
   Macmillan, 1972

GUIDES TO EDIBLE FUNGI

BADHAM, CHARLES D., *On the esculent funguses of England*, 1863

BRITTEN, JAMES, *Popular British fungi*, c. 1875

COOKE, M. C., *Edible and poisonous mushrooms*, 1894

GRIGSON, JANE, *The mushroom feast*, 1975

LOEWENFELD, CLAIRE, *Fungi*, 1956

MINISTRY OF AGRICULTURE, *Edible and poisonous fungi*, 1947

RAMSBOTTOM, JOHN, *Edible fungi*, 1943

RAMSBOTTOM, JOHN, *Mushrooms and toadstools*, 1953

SMITH, ALEXANDER H., *The mushroom hunter's field guide*, University
   of Michigan Press, 1971

ZEITLMAYR, LINUS, *Wild mushrooms*, 1968

ACKNOWLEDGEMENTS

I should like to thank J. E. Manners and the publishers of *Country Life* for permission to quote an extract from 'Truffle Hunting In England'.

Many people helped and gave advice during the preparation of this book. I should like to thank especially the Secretary and library staff of the Royal Horticultural Society, R. J. Kiel of the Publications Branch, and the library staff of the Ministry of Agriculture, Fisheries and Food; also A. A. Forsyth, author of the Ministry's excellent booklet on British Poisonous Plants, who gave me invaluable advice on the edibility of some entries; and Miss Pamela North, of the Pharmaceutical Society of Great Britain.

ILLUSTRATION CREDITS

The publishers wish to acknowledge the following artists:

Marjorie Blamey: pages 3, 16, 24–39, 42–49, 51 (right), 52, 53 (right), 54–56, 60–63, 66, 68–72, 74, 76–85, 86 (bottom), 87, 88, 89 (bottom), 90–92, 95, 96, 98, 99, 101 (top), 103, 104, 105 (top), 106 (top), 108, 109, 114–123, 125, 126 (bottom), 127 (left and centre), 128, 129 (top), 130 (centre and right), 131–133, 135, 136 (top), 138 (bottom), 141, 143, 145, 147, 149, 150, 151 (top), 152.

Jill Coombs: pages 101 (bottom), 126 (top), 129 (bottom), 130 (left), 137, 138 (top).

Victoria Goaman: page 139.

Sheila Hadley: pages 97, 102, 105 (bottom), 107, 110, 111, 112.

Marilyn Leader: pages 75, 93, 94.

David More: page 40.

Valerie Price: pages 64, 65, 67, 73, 89 (top), 124, 127 (right), 136 (bottom), 142, 144, 148, 151 (bottom).

Susannah Ray: pages 51 (left), 53 (left), 57, 59, 161, 162, 222, 224 (top), 225, 226, 227.

Fiona Silver: page 134.

Sue Wickison: pages 86 (top), 153.

John Wilkinson: pages 10, 34, 154–160, 163, 164, 169–218, 224 (bottom).

SOURCES

Collins Gem Guides

Fruits, Nuts and Berries and Conspicuous Seeds, Marjorie and Philip Blamey, Collins, 1984

Trees, David More and Alastair Fitter, Collins, 1980

Wild Flowers, Marjorie Blamey and Richard Fitter, Collins, 1980

The Seashore, Rosalind Fitter and Susanna Ray, Collins, 1984

Herbs for Cooking and Health, Christine Grey-Wilson and Jill Coombs, Collins, 1987

Garden Flowers, Christopher Grey-Wilson and Victoria Goaman, Collins, 1986

New Generation Guides

General Editor Sir David Attenborough

The Wild Flowers of Britain and Northern Europe, Alastair Fitter, Collins, 1987

The Fungi of Britain and Europe, Stefan Buczacki, Collins, 1989

INDEX